# THE NORWEGIAN RUNNING METHOD

How Elite Scandinavian Training Methods Build Speed, Endurance, and Consistency Without Overtraining or Burnout

ERIK LUNDQVIST

*A good coach can change a game. A great coach can change a life.*

— *John Wooden*

# Contents

# Introduction

Most runners aren't lazy. In fact, the opposite is usually true. They wake up early, squeeze in training before work, push through tired legs, and tell themselves that if they just try a little harder, the results will eventually follow. They chase new plans, new workouts, and new motivation, yet many still find themselves running the same race times year after year, dealing with recurring niggles, or feeling constantly tired without knowing exactly why.

This is one of the biggest frustrations in recreational running. You can be consistent, disciplined, and mentally tough, yet still feel like your progress has stalled. The problem is rarely a lack of effort. More often, it's how that effort is being used.

Modern running culture tends to celebrate intensity. Hard intervals, lung-burning tempo runs, and exhausting long runs are often seen as proof that training is working. If a session doesn't hurt, it can feel like it doesn't count. Over time, many runners fall into a pattern where they're training hard too often and easy not often enough, living in a gray zone that feels productive but quietly limits adaptation and increases fatigue.

At first, this approach can work. Fitness improves, race times drop, and confidence grows. But eventually, the gains slow. Legs feel heavy more often, recovery takes longer, and small aches start turning into longer layoffs. Instead of building momentum, training becomes a cycle of pushing, stalling, backing off, and starting again.

What's frustrating is that many runners assume this plateau is simply part of getting older or reaching their "natural limit." They accept that faster times are behind them and that staying healthy is the best they can hope for. In reality, many are leaving a huge amount of potential untapped, not because they aren't working hard enough, but because they are working hard in the wrong ways and at the wrong times.

This is where the Norwegian approach to training offers a very different perspective. Rather than chasing exhaustion, it focuses on controlling intensity, managing fatigue, and accumulating high-quality work that the body can actually absorb. The goal isn't to survive individual workouts, but to string together weeks and months of consistent, productive training.

Many runners assume that elite training systems only work for professionals with unlimited time and perfect recovery. That isn't the case. While world-class athletes may use advanced tools like double training days to increase total volume, the core principles behind their success are surprisingly simple and highly adaptable. When applied intelligently, the same ideas can help everyday runners train more effectively without adding more hours or more stress to their week.

Elite Scandinavian runners didn't arrive at this system by accident. It grew out of years of careful observation, data collection, and trial and error, all aimed at answering one simple question: how can athletes train at a high level every day without breaking down? The answer turned out to be surprisingly straightforward, but very different from how most recreational runners structure their training.

At its core, the Norwegian method shifts the focus away from dramatic workouts and toward sustainable progress. It prioritizes effort levels that stimulate improvement while keeping stress low enough that training can be repeated again and again. Over time, this creates a powerful compounding effect. Fitness builds steadily, confidence grows, and race performance improves without the constant cycle of fatigue and forced rest.

The encouraging part is that these principles are not reserved for professionals with endless recovery time and medical support. When adapted correctly, the same ideas can be used by everyday runners balancing training with work, family, and normal life stress. You don't need perfect conditions to train smarter. You just need a better framework for how intensity, volume, and recovery work together.

In the chapters that follow, we'll break down exactly what makes the Norwegian training system different, how threshold training really works, and how you can apply these principles to your own running, whether you're chasing a faster 5K, a stronger half marathon, or simply want to feel better and more consistent in your training.

As promising as this approach sounds, it raises an important question. If working harder isn't the answer, and exhaustion isn't the goal, then why do so many runners believe that more effort is always better? And how did training that constantly feels difficult become the default, even when it stops producing results? To understand why so many runners get stuck, we first need to look at how effort and improvement are often misunderstood.

# PART I
## Rethinking Intensity and Endurance

# ONE

# Why More Effort Doesn't Always Mean More Progress

Most runners are taught, directly or indirectly, that improvement comes from pushing harder. When training feels tough, it feels productive. When a workout leaves you gasping, drenched in sweat, and barely able to jog home, it feels like something important must have happened. This mindset is reinforced by race culture, social media, and even well-meaning training advice that praises grit and suffering as the main ingredients of success.

The problem is that the body doesn't adapt based on how painful a workout feels. It adapts based on the type of stress applied and whether that stress can be repeated consistently. A single brutal session might feel impressive, but if it compromises the quality of the next several days of training, the overall effect can actually be negative.

Many runners end up stuck in a pattern where most of their runs are harder than they should be, but not quite hard enough to trigger the strongest performance adaptations. Easy days drift into moderate effort. Hard days become survival efforts. Over time, this creates a constant background of fatigue that never fully clears, even though the runner is technically following a structured plan.

This middle ground is where progress quietly goes to stall. It feels challenging enough to satisfy the urge to work hard, but it doesn't provide the focused stimulus that truly builds aerobic efficiency or speed. At the same time, it drains recovery reserves, making it harder to absorb higher-quality training when it actually matters.

Ironically, runners who train this way often feel like they are always working, yet never quite fresh. Their workouts feel difficult, but their race performances fail to reflect the effort they are putting in. Instead of building fitness on top of fitness, they are constantly rebuilding from small doses of accumulated fatigue.

This is where the idea of "more effort equals more progress" begins to fall apart. Training stress only leads to improvement when it's followed by enough recovery to allow adaptation to take place. Without that recovery, effort simply becomes wear and tear. The body doesn't get stronger, it just gets more tired.

The Norwegian approach challenges this cycle by separating effort levels much more clearly. Easy days are truly easy. Hard days are carefully controlled rather than chaotic. Instead of chasing exhaustion, training is organized around intensities that stimulate improvement while still allowing the runner to show up ready to train again the next day.

This shift can feel uncomfortable at first, especially for runners who are used to measuring success by how drained they feel after a workout. But once training becomes more repeatable and recovery improves, progress starts to feel less dramatic in the moment and far more powerful over time.

To understand why controlling intensity is so important, we need to look more closely at what happens inside the body when effort rises and where the line exists between productive stress and unnecessary strain. That line is what coaches and physiologists refer to as threshold, and learning how to train around it is one of the most important skills a runner can develop.

# TWO

# The Problem With "Go Hard or Go Home" Training

If you spend any time around runners, online or in person, you'll notice how often training is talked about in terms of toughness. People swap stories about brutal intervals, miserable long runs, and how wrecked they felt afterward. There's an unspoken belief that if a session didn't hurt, it probably wasn't effective. Effort becomes a badge of honor, and exhaustion becomes proof of commitment.

This attitude isn't hard to understand. Running is uncomfortable by nature, and pushing through discomfort is part of the sport. Early improvements often come from simply doing more and trying harder. When a beginner runs their first fast intervals or finishes a tough long run, the body adapts quickly and results follow. That early success reinforces the idea that harder always means better.

The problem is that what works in the early stages of training does not work forever. As fitness improves, the body becomes more sensitive to how stress is applied. Workouts that once triggered strong adaptations begin to create more fatigue than benefit. But because runners are conditioned to associate effort with progress, they respond to slowing improvement by pushing even harder, not by questioning whether the structure of their training still makes sense.

Modern training culture makes this even worse. Apps reward intensity with glowing graphs and impressive-looking splits. Group runs often turn into informal races. Social media highlights dramatic workouts rather than quiet consistency. All of this nudges runners toward making more days feel hard, even when those days were supposed to be easy or moderate.

Over time, many runners end up training in a constant state of low-level fatigue. They're not injured, but they're rarely fresh. Easy runs feel sluggish. Hard runs feel harder than they should. Yet because they are still completing the workouts, they assume the system must be working, even as race performances stay flat or slowly decline.

Another issue with "go hard or go home" training is that it treats every hard session as equally valuable. In reality, different intensities create very different adaptations. Some efforts build aerobic efficiency. Others improve speed. Others simply accumulate fatigue. When too many sessions drift into a vague, uncomfortable middle zone, the body doesn't receive a clear signal about what it's supposed to improve.

This kind of training can feel busy and demanding without being particularly productive. Runners may log plenty of miles and complete plenty of tough sessions, yet still struggle to improve pace at sustainable effort levels. Worse, the constant strain increases the risk of injury, illness, and mental burnout, which can derail training entirely.

What makes this especially frustrating is that many runners blame themselves when progress slows. They assume they need more discipline, more motivation, or more grit. Rarely do they consider that the problem might be the structure of their training rather than their willingness to work.

The Norwegian approach challenges this culture by reframing what "hard work" actually means. Instead of measuring effort by how much a workout hurts, it measures effort by how well the body can absorb and repeat quality training over time. The focus shifts from dramatic sessions to reliable ones, from isolated hero days to steady weekly progress.

This doesn't mean avoiding discomfort or training cautiously all the time. It means being deliberate about when to push and when to protect recovery. Hard efforts still exist, but they are placed where they produce the greatest benefit, not where they simply satisfy the urge to suffer.

To understand how this different mindset translates into actual training, it helps to look at how elite Scandinavian programs organize their weeks and why their athletes can train at high levels without constantly breaking down. That structure, and the philosophy behind it, is what we'll explore next.

# THREE

# What Elite Scandinavian Runners Do Differently

If you watch elite runners train, especially those coming out of Scandinavian programs, one thing becomes clear very quickly: their training rarely looks chaotic. Sessions are controlled, paces are steady, and workouts often appear almost calm compared to the all-out efforts many recreational runners associate with "serious" training.

This can be surprising at first. People expect elite athletes to train in a constant state of exhaustion, pushing to the limit every day. In reality, most of their training is carefully organized so that hard work is targeted and recoverable. The goal is not to win every workout, but to build fitness in a way that allows high-quality training to be repeated again and again.

Rather than stacking intense sessions back to back, Scandinavian systems place a strong emphasis on rhythm. Easy days are truly easy. Quality days are clearly defined. This separation allows the body to respond fully to harder efforts without being dulled by lingering fatigue from previous sessions.

Another defining feature of these programs is how deliberately intensity is managed. Instead of guessing how hard a session should feel, athletes train within specific effort ranges designed to produce particular adaptations. This reduces the risk of drifting into that exhausting middle zone where effort is high but returns are limited.

Over time, this approach creates remarkable consistency. Athletes are able to complete more quality work across the week and across the season, not because they are tougher, but because their training is structured to support recovery rather than sabotage it. Injuries still happen, but they are far less frequent than in systems that rely heavily on repeated maximal efforts.

What truly sets these programs apart, however, is their long-term mindset. Training is not built around a single big race or a dramatic peak. It's built around steady development over months and years. Each training cycle builds on the last, gradually raising the level at which the athlete can operate without accumulating excessive fatigue.

This long-term view also changes how progress is measured. Instead of chasing personal bests in training sessions, success is judged by how stable paces feel, how well workouts are completed, and how quickly the body recovers afterward. These quieter signs of fitness often predict future race performance far better than any single impressive workout split.

Of course, elite runners also have access to resources that most people don't, including coaches, medical teams, and in some cases, laboratory testing to fine-tune intensity. But the foundation of their success is not technology. It's discipline around effort, patience with progression, and respect for recovery.

When these principles are stripped down to their essentials, they become surprisingly accessible. You don't need to train twice a day or follow a professional schedule to benefit from controlled intensity and repeatable training. What matters most is learning how to apply stress in a way that builds fitness instead of slowly eroding it.

The concept that sits at the center of this entire approach is something called threshold. It's the intensity level that allows runners to work hard enough to stimulate major aerobic improvements, while still staying in control of fatigue. Understanding what threshold actually is, and how to train around it, is the key to unlocking the Norwegian method in a practical, everyday setting.

# FOUR

# Understanding Threshold in Plain English

For all the attention threshold training gets in modern endurance coaching, the concept itself is often misunderstood. Many runners hear the word "threshold" and immediately think of a hard, lung-burning effort that leaves them counting down the minutes until the workout is over. Others confuse it with race pace or assume it's simply another name for running fast. In reality, threshold is neither easy nor extreme. It sits in a very specific and very useful middle ground.

Threshold refers to the highest intensity you can sustain while your body is still able to manage the fatigue being produced. At this effort level, your muscles are generating lactate, but your body is also clearing it efficiently enough that it doesn't rapidly build up. This balance allows you to hold the pace for a relatively long time compared to harder efforts, while still creating a strong stimulus for aerobic improvement.

From a runner's point of view, threshold feels "comfortably hard." Your breathing is deep and steady, but not panicked. You can't carry on a normal conversation, but you could manage short phrases if needed. Something like, "feels strong… but I couldn't keep this up all day," rather than, "I'm feeling great, let's chat about the weekend." Your legs feel engaged and working, but not out of control. Most importantly, the effort feels sustainable. You're working, but you're not fighting the pace.

This is very different from intervals designed to improve top-end speed or maximal oxygen uptake, where breathing becomes frantic and form starts to fall apart. Those efforts have their place, but they create much more fatigue and can't be repeated frequently without consequences. Threshold training, on the other hand, can be performed multiple times per week when managed correctly, which is why it plays such a central role in Norwegian-style systems.

One of the most common mistakes runners make is turning threshold runs into something harder than they need to be. It's easy to drift just a little faster, especially when feeling good, and that small increase in pace can push the body into a very different stress zone. What should have been a productive, repeatable workout becomes a session that demands extra recovery and disrupts the rest of the week.

When this happens repeatedly, runners unknowingly shift much of their training into an intensity range that feels productive but delivers poor long-term results. The workouts feel hard, yet the aerobic adaptations are less efficient, and recovery is compromised. This is one of the main reasons people train consistently but still struggle to improve race performance.

The Norwegian method places so much emphasis on threshold because it offers an unusually efficient return on investment. At this intensity, runners can accumulate a large amount of quality running that strengthens the aerobic system, improves fatigue resistance, and raises the pace that can be sustained during races. Over time, threshold pace becomes faster even though the effort level feels the same, which is exactly what endurance training is meant to achieve.

Another benefit of threshold training is how predictable it is. Because the effort is controlled, runners can plan sessions more accurately and monitor progress more reliably. Instead of guessing whether a workout was effective based on how exhausted they feel afterward, they can track how stable their pace and heart rate remain across repeats and across weeks.

It's also important to understand that threshold is not a fixed pace. It shifts with fitness, fatigue, heat, sleep, stress, and many other factors. That's why learning to recognize the effort level is more important than chasing exact numbers. On some days, threshold might feel slower than expected, and forcing the pace higher only defeats the purpose of the session.

This focus on effort rather than ego is what allows threshold training to remain sustainable. When runners learn to respect that boundary between productive stress and excessive strain, they gain the ability to train hard often, rather than extremely once in a while.

In the Norwegian system, threshold is not just another workout type. It becomes the backbone of weekly training, carefully balanced with easy aerobic running and occasional higher-intensity sessions. How that balance is achieved, and how threshold sessions are arranged across the week, is what truly separates this method from more traditional training approaches.

In the next chapter, we'll look at how threshold fits into the broader picture of aerobic development, and why building endurance is not just about running longer, but about running smarter at the right intensities.

# FIVE

# Why Staying Just Below the
# Red Line Changes Everything

When runners talk about "pushing the pace," they usually imagine that the harder they work, the more fitness they gain. It seems logical. If running at a certain speed is good, then running a little faster must be even better. The problem is that the body does not respond to stress in a straight line. Small increases in intensity can produce very large increases in fatigue, and that imbalance can quietly undermine training.

There's a point during hard running where effort begins to rise faster than fitness. Below this point, the body can manage the stress and adapt. Above it, fatigue starts to accumulate more rapidly, recovery slows, and the same workout becomes much harder to repeat. This tipping point is what many runners experience as the moment a run stops feeling controlled and starts feeling like a fight.

Staying just below that red line allows runners to apply stress in a way that builds fitness without constantly draining their recovery reserves. The aerobic system receives a strong signal to improve, but the muscles and nervous system are not pushed into deep fatigue. This balance is what makes it possible to train hard, recover well, and return to quality sessions again within a few days.

When runners cross that line too often, even by a small margin, the cost shows up in subtle ways. Paces begin to drift downward on easy days. Workouts start to feel harder than they should. Sleep may be disrupted. Motivation can dip. None of these signs alone seem alarming, but together they indicate that the body is spending more time repairing damage than building fitness.

Over time, this leads to an unfortunate trade-off. Runners may feel like they are always training hard, yet they are unable to accumulate enough high-quality work across the week to drive meaningful improvement. The effort is high, but the consistency is low, and consistency is what ultimately determines long-term progress.

By contrast, runners who stay just under the red line are able to stack productive training days together. They complete threshold sessions that challenge the aerobic system without wrecking their legs. They recover more quickly between workouts. They maintain steadier training rhythms across weeks instead of bouncing between exhaustion and rest.

This is where the real advantage of threshold-focused training appears. It doesn't rely on isolated breakthroughs or peak efforts. It relies on steady accumulation. Each session builds slightly on the last, and over time, the pace that once felt challenging becomes manageable. Then that new pace becomes the baseline for the next round of improvement.

This approach also creates a psychological shift. Training becomes something that feels repeatable and predictable rather than something that constantly demands mental toughness just to get through it. Runners begin to trust the process instead of questioning whether they are doing enough after every workout.

The Norwegian system is built around protecting this balance. It accepts that pushing above threshold has its place, but it treats those efforts as specific tools rather than default settings. Most of the meaningful development happens at intensities that allow athletes to train frequently and recover quickly.

Understanding why this balance matters requires a closer look at what is actually happening inside the body when effort increases and fatigue begins to rise. In the next section, we'll explore how lactate is produced and cleared, and why improving this process is one of the most powerful ways to raise sustainable running speed.

# PART II

# The Physiology That Makes It Work

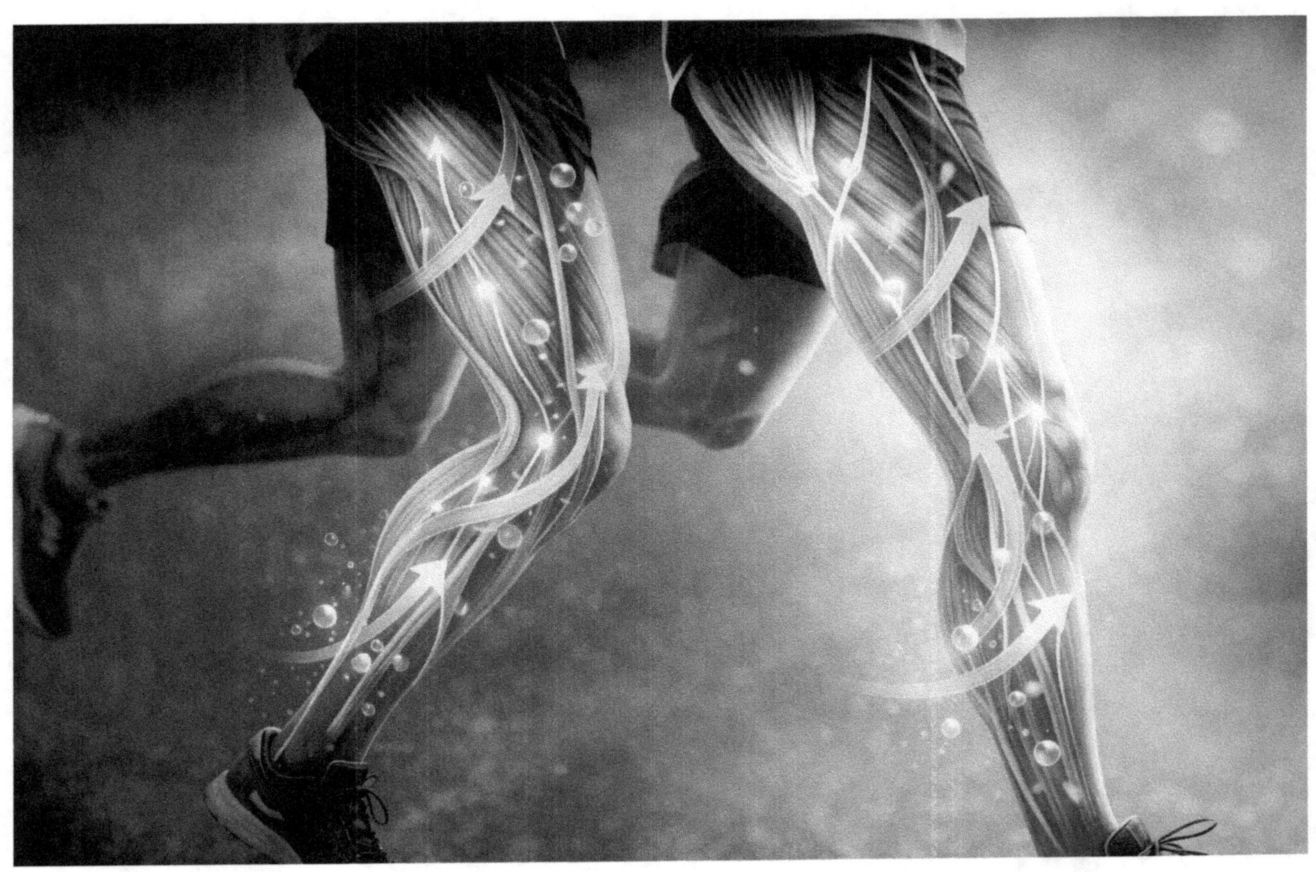

# SIX

# The Physiology That Makes It Work

For many runners, the word "lactate" has a bad reputation. It's often blamed for burning legs, slowing pace, and that heavy feeling that creeps in during hard efforts. Because of this, lactate is commonly seen as something the body should avoid producing. In reality, lactate is not the problem. It's simply part of how the body creates energy when intensity increases, and it also plays an important role in helping muscles keep working.

Any time you run faster than a very easy jog, your muscles begin producing lactate. This is normal and unavoidable. Lactate is created when the body breaks down carbohydrates to produce energy more quickly than oxygen alone can support. Far from being useless waste, lactate can be transported to other muscles and even back to the heart and liver, where it can be reused as fuel.

The issue is not whether lactate is produced, but whether it's cleared at roughly the same rate. When production and clearance stay in balance, effort can be sustained for long periods. When production rises faster than clearance, lactate begins to accumulate, and fatigue increases much more quickly. This is when running starts to feel harder with each passing minute, even if pace stays the same.

Threshold sits very close to the point where this balance begins to shift. At or just below threshold, the body is working hard, but it's still keeping up with the demands being placed on it. Just above threshold, that balance starts to tip, and fatigue begins to rise much faster. This is why small changes in pace can lead to very different recovery needs and training outcomes.

Training near threshold improves the body's ability to both tolerate and clear lactate. Muscles become more efficient at using oxygen, transporting fuel, and shuttling lactate to where it can be reused. Over time, this allows runners to operate at faster speeds before fatigue begins to build. In practical terms, this means race pace starts to feel more controlled, and the point at which running becomes uncomfortable is pushed farther down the road.

When runners spend too much time above this level, they still improve certain aspects of fitness, but the cost is much higher. Recovery takes longer, quality training becomes harder to repeat, and the risk of injury increases. Occasional high-intensity work can be useful, but it cannot form the foundation of a system built on consistency.

The Norwegian approach recognizes that improving lactate management is one of the most powerful ways to raise sustainable speed. By focusing a large portion of quality training around intensities that challenge the aerobic system without overwhelming it, athletes can accumulate far more productive work across the week and across the season.

This doesn't mean avoiding discomfort. Threshold training is still demanding, and it still requires focus and discipline. The difference is that the stress is applied in a way that the body can recover from quickly, allowing adaptation to take place instead of simply accumulating fatigue.

Understanding lactate helps explain why the Norwegian method emphasizes controlled intensity and repeatable sessions rather than constant maximal efforts. It's not about avoiding hard work. It's about placing that work where it produces the greatest long-term return.

In the next chapter, we'll look more closely at the difference between aerobic power and aerobic capacity, and why building both matters for runners who want to improve not just how fast they can run, but how long they can hold strong paces during races.

# SEVEN

# Aerobic Power vs. Aerobic Capacity and Why Both Matter

When runners talk about fitness, they often treat it as a single quality. You're either "fit" or you're not. In reality, endurance performance depends on several different systems working together, and understanding the difference between them helps explain why some types of training feel powerful but don't always translate into better race results.

One useful way to think about aerobic fitness is to separate it into two components: aerobic power and aerobic capacity. Aerobic power refers to how much oxygen your body can use at its maximum. This is often described as $VO_2$ max, and it represents the ceiling of your aerobic system. The higher this ceiling, the more energy you can produce when running hard.

Aerobic capacity, on the other hand, refers to how much of that power you can actually sustain over time. It determines how close you can operate to your maximum without fatiguing quickly. Two runners may have similar aerobic power, but if one can hold a higher percentage of that power for longer, that runner will perform better in races.

Many traditional training programs place heavy emphasis on improving aerobic power through high-intensity intervals. Sessions like hard hill repeats or long, fast intervals push the cardiovascular system near its limits and can raise the ceiling of what the body is capable of. These workouts are demanding and often feel very productive, which is why runners tend to gravitate toward them.

The problem is that raising the ceiling does not automatically improve how long you can stay near it. Without sufficient work at controlled, sustainable intensities, runners may increase their top-end capacity but struggle to translate that into faster race paces. They can go very hard for short periods, but they cannot hold strong speeds comfortably for the duration of an event.

Threshold training plays a key role in improving aerobic capacity. By spending time near the highest intensity that can be sustained without rapid fatigue, the body learns to operate efficiently at demanding paces. This raises the percentage of aerobic power that can be used during races, which is often more important than increasing maximum capacity alone.

This is one of the reasons Norwegian systems emphasize frequent threshold work. Instead of focusing primarily on raising the ceiling, they focus on lifting the floor closer to that ceiling. Over time, race pace becomes a smaller fraction of maximum effort, making it easier to sustain speed when it matters most.

High-intensity training still has a place, especially for improving short-distance performance and overall cardiovascular strength. But when used too often, it can interfere with recovery and reduce the amount of quality work that can be completed in the rest of the week. The Norwegian approach treats these sessions as supplements rather than foundations.

By prioritizing aerobic capacity through controlled intensity, runners are able to develop fatigue resistance, maintain form late in races, and recover more quickly between training sessions. This creates a training environment where consistency is not just possible, but expected.

The balance between aerobic power and aerobic capacity is what allows runners to be both fast and durable. Focusing too heavily on one at the expense of the other often leads to impressive workouts but disappointing race performances.

In the next chapter, we'll explore why controlled intensity not only improves endurance, but also leads to faster running speeds over time, even when workouts don't feel extreme.

# EIGHT

# Why Controlled Intensity Builds Faster Runners

It's easy to assume that to run faster, you must regularly train at very fast speeds. While speed-focused workouts do play a role in development, they aren't the primary driver of sustainable race performance for most distance runners. In fact, much of what allows runners to improve pace comes from training that feels controlled rather than extreme.

One of the key reasons controlled intensity works so well is that it improves running economy. Economy refers to how much energy you use at a given pace. When your body becomes more efficient, you can run faster without needing to work harder. Threshold training encourages this efficiency by reinforcing smooth mechanics and stable pacing under moderate fatigue, which closely resembles the conditions of real racing.

At controlled intensities, runners are also able to maintain better form. Stride stays relaxed, posture remains stable, and unnecessary tension is reduced. When training consistently reinforces these movement patterns, they become automatic. During races, this translates into better speed maintenance when fatigue begins to set in.

Another benefit of controlled training is how it improves pacing awareness. Runners who frequently operate near threshold develop a strong sense of what sustainable effort feels like. This makes them less likely to start races too fast and more capable of holding steady splits throughout the event. Even small improvements in pacing strategy can produce meaningful gains in finishing time.

Controlled threshold work also improves how muscles recruit and coordinate fibers during prolonged efforts. Instead of relying heavily on fast-twitch fibers that fatigue quickly, the body becomes better at sustaining work through more fatigue-resistant muscle fibers. This allows runners to maintain speed deeper into races without the dramatic slowdown that often follows overly aggressive early pacing.

Importantly, this type of training can be performed more often without compromising recovery. Because fatigue remains manageable, runners can accumulate more total quality minutes across the week. Over time, this repeated exposure to productive effort levels builds a strong aerobic base that supports faster paces across all race distances.

This is why runners following threshold-based systems often report that their speed improves even though they rarely feel like they are "hammering" workouts. Instead of chasing peak intensity, they are quietly expanding the range of paces they can sustain comfortably.

High-intensity sessions still have value, particularly for sharpening speed and improving aerobic power. But without a strong foundation of controlled aerobic work, those sessions provide limited benefit and can even disrupt progress by increasing fatigue and injury risk.

The Norwegian method prioritizes controlled intensity because it creates an environment where speed emerges as a byproduct of efficient, repeatable training rather than as the result of constant maximal efforts. Faster running becomes something that develops naturally as the aerobic system strengthens and fatigue resistance improves.

In the next chapter, we'll look at how fatigue accumulates across days and weeks, and why managing this invisible load is just as important as choosing the right workout intensities.

# NINE

# Fatigue, Recovery, and the Hidden Cost of Overreaching

Most runners understand that hard training requires recovery. What many underestimate is how easily fatigue can accumulate even when no single workout feels extreme. Instead of coming from one dramatic session, overreaching usually develops slowly, through a series of days that are just a little too demanding and a little too close together.

When training stress outpaces recovery, the body shifts into a state where it spends more time repairing damage than building new fitness. At first, this isn't obvious. Workouts may still get done, and motivation may remain high. But subtle signs begin to appear. Legs feel heavier during easy runs. Warm-ups take longer to feel comfortable. Paces that once felt manageable start to feel harder than expected.

Because these changes happen gradually, many runners respond by pushing more, not less. They assume the solution to feeling flat is to work harder or add intensity, which only increases the recovery debt they're already carrying. Over time, this creates a cycle where training feels increasingly difficult while performance stays the same or even declines.

Another issue with chronic fatigue is that it affects how the nervous system controls movement. Coordination becomes less precise, posture becomes harder to maintain, and muscles begin compensating for one another. This increases the risk of small aches turning into real injuries, especially in areas that are already under stress like the calves, achilles, knees, and hips.

Sleep, nutrition, and life stress also play a role in how well runners recover, but training intensity is the variable most within a runner's control. When intensity is not managed carefully, even moderate training volumes can become overwhelming over time. This is why some runners feel constantly tired despite not running particularly high mileage.

The Norwegian approach aims to reduce this hidden fatigue by tightly controlling how much stress is applied in each quality session. By keeping most demanding efforts in a range that the body can recover from quickly, athletes protect their ability to train consistently rather than constantly oscillating between hard days and forced rest.

This doesn't mean eliminating fatigue entirely. Productive training still creates stress, and feeling tired after hard sessions is normal. The difference is that recovery happens within a predictable window, allowing the next planned workout to be executed with good quality instead of being compromised by lingering exhaustion.

When fatigue is managed properly, runners begin to notice changes not just in performance, but in how training feels overall. Easy days feel easier. Hard days feel challenging but controlled. There is a sense that training is building rather than simply draining energy reserves.

Perhaps the most dangerous aspect of overreaching is that it often feels like commitment. Runners take pride in pushing through tired legs and showing up no matter what. While mental toughness is an important part of racing, applying it every day in training can backfire by preventing the body from adapting fully.

Sustainable improvement depends on applying stress that the body can respond to, then allowing enough recovery for that response to take place. Without that balance, effort turns into wear rather than growth.

In the next chapter, we'll look at why consistency, not intensity, is the true multiplier of long-term performance, and how protecting training rhythm often matters more than any individual workout.

# TEN

# Consistency as the Real Performance Multiplier

When runners look back on their best performances, they often remember specific workouts that made them feel strong or confident. But those single sessions are rarely what produced the result. More often, it was the accumulation of many solid weeks of training, each one building quietly on the last, that created the fitness needed to perform well on race day.

Consistency is what allows all the physiological adaptations discussed so far to actually take hold. Improvements in lactate clearance, aerobic efficiency, and fatigue resistance do not happen overnight. They develop gradually through repeated exposure to the right kinds of stress, followed by adequate recovery. When training is frequently interrupted by excessive fatigue, illness, or injury, those adaptations never have the chance to fully compound.

This is why systems built around repeatable intensity tend to outperform those built around extreme effort. If a runner can complete quality training week after week, even if individual sessions feel less dramatic, the total amount of productive work over a season becomes much greater. That cumulative effect is what drives meaningful performance gains.

Consistency also improves how well runners learn their own bodies. When training rhythms are stable, it becomes easier to recognize what different effort levels feel like, how long recovery normally takes, and when something is off. This awareness allows for smarter adjustments and reduces the risk of pushing through warning signs that could lead to setbacks.

Another advantage of consistent training is psychological. Progress feels more predictable, and confidence grows as runners see steady improvement instead of sporadic peaks and crashes. Training becomes something that fits into life rather than something that constantly demands recovery from it.

The Norwegian approach is designed around protecting this rhythm. By emphasizing controlled intensity and careful placement of harder sessions, it reduces the chances that a single workout will disrupt the entire week. Over time, this creates a training environment where showing up healthy and ready to train becomes the norm rather than the exception.

This doesn't mean that every week feels easy or that progress is perfectly linear. Fatigue still fluctuates, and setbacks still happen. But when training is structured to prioritize sustainability, those setbacks are usually smaller and easier to recover from, allowing momentum to continue rather than collapse.

Ultimately, the real advantage of the Norwegian method is not that it produces occasional breakthroughs, but that it makes steady improvement far more likely. When runners protect consistency, they give themselves the best chance to benefit from every aspect of training, from threshold work to long runs to occasional high-intensity efforts.

With this foundation in place, we can now look at how these principles are organized into actual training weeks. In the next section, we'll explore how threshold sessions are arranged, what double threshold really means in practice, and how these ideas can be adapted for runners who don't have the time or recovery resources of elite athletes.

PART III
Inside the Norwegian Training System

# ELEVEN

# Inside the Norwegian Training System - Double Threshold Training

When people first hear about double threshold training, it often sounds extreme. Two hard sessions in one day can easily be mistaken for overtraining or unnecessary punishment. This misunderstanding has led many runners to either dismiss the method entirely or attempt to copy it in ways that quickly lead to exhaustion and injury.

In reality, double threshold training is not about pushing harder. It's about managing workload more intelligently. The idea is to divide a day's quality training into two controlled sessions rather than forcing all of that stress into one longer, more fatiguing workout.

Both sessions are performed at or just below threshold, not above it. The effort is challenging but stable, and neither workout should leave the runner completely drained. The purpose is to accumulate a larger amount of productive aerobic work while keeping fatigue low enough that recovery remains manageable.

For elite runners, this structure allows a high total volume of threshold training across the week without relying on extremely long or intense single sessions. Instead of one big effort that creates significant muscle damage and nervous system fatigue, the load is spread across the day, reducing the stress of each individual bout.

What double threshold is not is two race-pace or faster workouts stacked together. It's not interval training in the traditional sense, and it's not meant to test mental toughness. If either session feels like a maximal effort, the intensity is too high and the purpose of the method is lost.

This distinction is critical, because many runners who try to replicate double threshold days end up performing two moderately hard workouts that are both above threshold. That combination dramatically increases fatigue and recovery needs, which is the opposite of what the Norwegian system is designed to achieve.

Another common misconception is that double threshold is required for the method to work. It is not. Double threshold is simply one way elites increase total quality volume when they're already training at very high levels and have exceptional recovery capacity. The underlying principle is not the number of sessions per day, but the careful control of intensity and the frequent exposure to productive aerobic stress.

For everyday runners, attempting true double threshold days is rarely necessary and often impractical. Most people are balancing training with work, family, and normal life stress, which already places demands on recovery. Adding a second quality session in the same day can quickly tip the balance toward chronic fatigue.

This is why the Norwegian philosophy is better thought of as threshold-focused rather than double-threshold dependent. The method works because it prioritizes repeatable, controlled intensity across the week, not because it requires multiple sessions in a single day.

Understanding this helps shift the focus away from copying elite schedules and toward applying elite principles in a way that fits individual circumstances. The goal is not to train like a professional, but to train in a way that produces steady improvement without unnecessary breakdown.

In the next chapter, we'll look more closely at why splitting sessions can be useful for those who can handle it, and what it teaches us about how training stress and recovery interact, even when we only train once per day.

# TWELVE

# Why Splitting Sessions Works Better Than One Big Workout

When most runners think about a hard training day, they imagine one demanding session that pushes them close to their limits. The assumption is that if a workout is challenging enough, it must be effective. But from a physiological standpoint, how stress is distributed can matter just as much as how much stress is applied.

Long, intense workouts create two types of fatigue at the same time. They place heavy metabolic demands on the aerobic system, and they also produce significant muscle damage and nervous system strain. While both of these stresses can stimulate adaptation, they also increase recovery time. The longer and harder a session becomes, the more it shifts from being primarily aerobic to being mechanically and neurologically exhausting.

Splitting training into smaller, controlled sessions changes this balance. Each workout still challenges the aerobic system, but the mechanical and neuromuscular damage is lower. This allows the body to recover more quickly, even though the total amount of quality work across the day may be higher.

This is the core logic behind double threshold days for elite runners. Instead of doing one long threshold workout that leaves the legs heavy for days, they perform two shorter sessions that are both demanding but manageable. The aerobic stimulus remains high, but the cost to recovery is reduced.

Another advantage of shorter, controlled sessions is that pacing and technique are easier to maintain. When fatigue rises too high, form deteriorates and effort becomes inefficient. By keeping sessions within manageable limits, runners reinforce better movement patterns and more stable pacing, which improves how that effort translates to race performance.

From a recovery perspective, splitting stress also prevents what could be called "training bottlenecks." When one huge workout overwhelms the system, it can compromise the next several days of training. When stress is distributed more evenly, each session fits into the larger weekly rhythm instead of dominating it.

For non-elite runners, the takeaway isn't that they should start training twice a day. The takeaway is that piling all quality work into a single massive session is rarely the most effective option. Similar benefits can often be achieved by shortening hard workouts, keeping intensity controlled, and allowing enough easy running between quality days to protect recovery.

This is why Norwegian-style programs tend to feature frequent, moderate threshold sessions rather than occasional brutal ones. The goal isn't to see how much pain can be tolerated in a single day, but how much productive training can be completed across the entire week.

When training is organized this way, runners often notice that they can handle more quality work overall without feeling constantly depleted. Instead of needing several days to recover from one demanding session, they are able to train consistently with only small fluctuations in fatigue.

This principle also explains why stacking very hard workouts back-to-back is so risky. Even if each session looks reasonable on its own, the combined stress can exceed what the body can recover from in time, leading to a slow decline in performance and motivation.

Ultimately, splitting stress, whether across two sessions in one day for elites or across several controlled sessions in a week for recreational runners, allows training to remain productive rather than destructive. It's one of the key ways the Norwegian system protects long-term development while still driving performance forward.

In the next chapter, we'll look at how often threshold training should actually appear in a typical week, and how to balance it with easy running and other types of workouts.

# How Often Threshold Should Actually Appear in Your Week

Once runners understand the value of threshold training, the next natural question is how often it should be done. Some assume that because threshold is safer than maximal intensity, more must always be better. Others worry that doing it too frequently will still lead to fatigue and injury. The answer, as with most training questions, depends on how well intensity is controlled and how much recovery is built into the rest of the week.

Elite Norwegian athletes often perform threshold training several times per week, and sometimes even on multiple sessions in the same day. These examples are not meant to suggest that recreational runners should train like professionals, but to show how strongly Norwegian systems prioritize frequent, controlled aerobic stress and careful distribution of intensity.

To understand how this works at the highest level, it helps to look at how athletes like Jakob Ingebrigtsen structure their training weeks. In many Norwegian systems, threshold work is organized around two key days each week, commonly on Tuesday and Thursday. On these days, runners complete two controlled threshold sessions, one in the morning and one in the afternoon or evening. Each session typically includes around 25 to 30 minutes of total threshold running, broken into repeats such as 5 × 1.25 miles (2,000 meters) in the morning and 10 × 0.62 miles (1,000 meters) in the afternoon, with short recoveries that keep effort steady rather than spiking. Across the full day, total threshold time can reach 50 to 60 minutes, but it's split in a way that keeps each individual session manageable and repeatable.

The rest of the week is built to support these demanding days rather than compete with them. Easy aerobic runs usually fill Monday and Friday, along with additional easy mileage on parts of the weekend. Sunday is often reserved for a longer endurance run at relaxed intensity. On some weeks, athletes may also include a supplemental session such as hill repeats or short high-intensity intervals, often placed on Saturday. These are carefully controlled so they don't interfere with recovery from the threshold work earlier in the week. Even at the elite level, most training remains easy, with demanding efforts concentrated into specific, well-planned sessions.

One published example of a typical elite week shows Tuesday featuring about 60 minutes of total threshold running split between morning and afternoon sessions, Thursday including roughly 50 minutes of threshold work in the same split format, Saturday combining hill work with a short block of controlled aerobic running, and Sunday devoted to a longer steady run. Easy runs fill in the remaining days. This structure highlights how carefully intensity is managed, even for world-class athletes, and how much emphasis is placed on protecting recovery and maintaining training rhythm.

Research on elite Norwegian middle and long-distance runners competing in events from 1,500 meters to 10,000 meters supports this pattern. Weekly mileage in these groups often ranges from roughly 75 to 110 miles (120 to 180 kilometers), with the vast majority of that distance completed at low intensity. During base and development phases, athletes commonly perform two to four threshold sessions per week, sometimes split across days, while only one or two sessions are dedicated to higher-intensity work aimed at improving aerobic power. The overall emphasis remains on accumulating large amounts of productive aerobic training without overwhelming recovery systems.

These examples aren't meant to suggest that recreational runners should train twice per day or run elite-level mileage. They simply illustrate how strongly Norwegian systems prioritize frequent, controlled aerobic stress and careful distribution of intensity. The success of this method does not come from extreme workouts, but from repeatable training that can be absorbed week after week.

For most recreational runners, this same principle translates into one or two threshold-focused sessions per week, supported by easy running and long aerobic efforts. Instead of splitting sessions across the day, the focus becomes placing quality workouts far enough apart that each can be performed with stable pacing, good form, and full recovery afterward. The structure changes, but the philosophy remains the same: train hard often enough to improve, but not so hard that recovery and consistency are sacrificed.

For many runners, this might mean one threshold workout midweek and another incorporated into a long run or steady aerobic session on the weekend.

More advanced runners, especially those with higher weekly mileage and good recovery habits, may benefit from adding a third controlled session in certain training phases. This does not necessarily mean adding another full workout, but could involve extending a long run with a sustained moderate effort or including shorter threshold segments within otherwise easy runs.

The key factor is not the number of sessions, but how well each one fits into the larger weekly rhythm. If threshold days leave runners unable to complete subsequent workouts with good quality, frequency is too high or intensity is too aggressive.

Another important consideration is that threshold training shouldn't crowd out easy running. Easy aerobic miles play a critical role in building endurance, supporting recovery, and strengthening connective tissue. Without enough low-intensity volume, even well-designed threshold programs can become unsustainable.

This is why Norwegian-style training weeks tend to follow a predictable pattern: quality sessions are clearly separated by easy days, and easy days are kept truly easy. This separation allows runners to train hard when it matters and recover fully when it does not.

It's also important to recognize that threshold frequency should change throughout the season. During base-building phases, threshold may appear less often as runners focus on building aerobic volume. During specific preparation phases, threshold work becomes more prominent as race pace and endurance are refined. After races, threshold frequency may drop again to allow for recovery and rebuilding.

Trying to maintain the same level of intensity year-round is one of the fastest ways to stagnate. Effective training systems ebb and flow, adjusting stress to match the body's current capacity and goals.

Ultimately, threshold training should feel like something that strengthens your week, not something that dominates it. When placed correctly, it enhances both fitness and confidence. When overused, it quickly becomes another source of fatigue.

In the next chapter, we'll look at how threshold sessions fit alongside easy mileage, long runs, and other types of workouts, and how to balance all of these elements into a sustainable training week.

# FOURTEEN

# Balancing Easy Miles With Quality Work

One of the biggest mistakes runners make when trying to train more seriously is turning too many days into moderate efforts. These runs don't feel easy, but they also aren't true workouts. They sit in an uncomfortable middle zone where fatigue builds steadily while the training benefit remains limited. Over time, this pattern makes it difficult to recover properly and harder to perform well on quality days.

Easy running plays a critical role in endurance development, even though it often feels too slow to be productive. At low intensities, the body is able to increase blood flow to muscles, strengthen connective tissue, and improve aerobic efficiency without placing heavy stress on the nervous system or muscles. These adaptations support harder training by improving the body's ability to handle volume and recover between demanding sessions.

When easy days are kept truly easy, they create a contrast that makes quality workouts more effective. Hard days feel sharper, pacing is easier to control, and recovery between intervals improves. When easy days are run too fast, that contrast disappears, and runners begin carrying fatigue into sessions that are supposed to be high quality.

This is one of the reasons Norwegian-style systems are so strict about separating intensities. Instead of allowing most runs to drift into moderate territory, they keep the majority of mileage at very relaxed effort. This protects the ability to train hard when it matters and prevents cumulative fatigue from quietly taking over.

Many runners struggle with this because easy pace can feel uncomfortable at first, especially if they are used to running every session at a similar effort. Slowing down may feel like a step backward, but in reality it allows the body to absorb more total training and improve more steadily over time.

Balancing easy and hard days also helps protect against injury. Lower-intensity running places less stress on joints and tendons, allowing tissues to adapt gradually to increasing mileage. When too many sessions are moderately hard, tissues are constantly under strain, increasing the likelihood that small issues turn into chronic problems.

Another benefit of easy days is that they support mental recovery. Training becomes less draining when not every run feels like a test. This makes it easier to stay motivated and consistent across long training cycles, which is far more important than pushing through short bursts of extreme effort.

In practical terms, most runners benefit from following a simple rhythm: quality days are clearly defined and limited, while the majority of runs are comfortable enough that breathing remains relaxed and form feels natural. If a runner cannot recover fully before the next planned workout, it's often a sign that easy days are not actually easy.

This balance also allows long runs to serve multiple purposes. Some long runs remain entirely easy, building endurance and durability. Others may include controlled segments near threshold, especially as race preparation approaches. What matters is that these harder portions are planned and limited, not the result of drifting into harder effort for the entire run.

Ultimately, easy running is not wasted time. It's what allows quality training to be effective and sustainable. Without enough truly easy mileage, threshold sessions lose much of their benefit, and training becomes a constant struggle against fatigue rather than a steady process of improvement.

In the next chapter, we'll look at where speed work, hill training, and higher-intensity intervals fit within the Norwegian framework, and how to use them without undermining the consistency that makes the system work.

# FIFTEEN

# Where Speed Work and the 4x4 Method Fit In

While threshold training forms the backbone of the Norwegian approach, it's not the only type of training used. Speed work, hill sessions, and high-intensity intervals still play a role, particularly for improving aerobic power and neuromuscular sharpness. The key difference is that these sessions are treated as tools, not as the foundation of the entire program.

High-intensity training raises the ceiling of what the aerobic system can handle. It improves how much oxygen the body can use at maximum effort and strengthens the cardiovascular system's ability to deliver oxygen to working muscles. This type of training is especially important for runners competing in shorter track races like the 800 meters and 1,500 meters, where aerobic power and speed play a major role. For 5K, 10K, and half-marathon runners, high-intensity sessions like 4×4 are better used sparingly, mainly to sharpen fitness, while threshold and steady aerobic training remain the primary drivers of performance.

One of the most well-known Norwegian interval formats is the 4×4 method. This involves four repeats of four minutes at high but controlled intensity, with a few minutes of easy recovery between efforts. The goal is to spend meaningful time near maximal aerobic output without turning the session into an all-out sprint workout.

The intensity of 4×4 intervals should feel hard, but sustainable across all four repeats. Breathing will be heavy, but pace should remain stable. If speed drops sharply or form deteriorates significantly, the effort is likely too aggressive. When performed correctly, the workout challenges aerobic power without creating excessive muscle damage.

In Norwegian systems, sessions like 4×4 are used sparingly and strategically. They are often placed in phases where increasing top-end aerobic capacity is a priority, such as early in a training cycle or during race-specific preparation. They are not performed every week year-round, and they are rarely stacked alongside heavy threshold weeks.

This is where many runners go wrong when trying to copy elite methods. They add intense interval workouts on top of already demanding training schedules, assuming more intensity will accelerate progress. In reality, this often compromises recovery and reduces the quality of threshold sessions, which are far more important for building sustainable race fitness.

Speed work and hills can also serve as technical tools. Short uphill repeats, strides, and relaxed fast running improve coordination, leg stiffness, and running mechanics without requiring long periods of maximal effort. These sessions add variety and help maintain efficiency, but they don't replace the need for aerobic development.

Short bouts of faster running, often called strides, are one of the simplest ways to maintain speed and efficiency without adding significant fatigue. These are brief accelerations lasting 15 to 25 seconds, performed at fast but relaxed pace, usually after easy runs. Because they are short and fully controlled, they improve neuromuscular coordination and reinforce efficient mechanics without placing meaningful stress on the aerobic system or requiring long recovery.

Hill sprints serve a similar purpose, with the added benefit of building strength and stiffness in the lower legs. Performed on moderate slopes for just 8 to 12 seconds, they encourage powerful but controlled movement while reducing impact forces compared to flat sprints. When kept very short and separated by full recovery, hill sprints improve running economy and resilience without interfering with threshold training or long runs.

The key with both strides and hills is that they should feel sharp, not exhausting. They are not workouts meant to leave runners breathless or sore, and they should never compromise recovery for the next day's training. When used correctly, they support the main aerobic work by keeping the body efficient and responsive, rather than replacing threshold sessions or long endurance efforts.

In practical terms, this usually means keeping volume very low. For strides, most runners do well with four to eight repetitions of 15 to 25 seconds, focusing on relaxed speed and smooth form, with full easy recovery between each effort. For hill sprints, four to ten short repeats of eight to twelve seconds on a moderate incline are enough to build strength and coordination, provided recovery is complete and the effort remains controlled rather than all-out. These sessions should leave runners feeling more awake and coordinated, not fatigued. If legs feel heavy afterward or the next day's training is affected, volume or intensity is likely too high.

In Norwegian-style systems, these types of speed elements are treated as maintenance tools rather than primary training drivers. They help preserve movement quality and running mechanics while the bulk of fitness is built through controlled aerobic work. This allows athletes to stay fast without sacrificing the consistency that drives long-term improvement.

Within the Norwegian framework, truly high-intensity training is carefully balanced against threshold and easy running to prevent fatigue from accumulating across the week. When overall fatigue is low and training rhythm is stable, adding occasional high-intensity work can enhance performance. When fatigue is already elevated, adding more intensity usually does more harm than good.

For recreational runners, the most practical approach is to treat these workouts as optional enhancements rather than mandatory components of every week. Many runners can make excellent progress using primarily threshold sessions, long runs, and easy mileage, adding speed work only during specific phases of training or when preparing for shorter races.

The main goal is not to eliminate intensity, but to ensure it supports rather than disrupts the broader training system. When high-intensity sessions are placed thoughtfully, they can complement threshold training and improve overall performance. When they are added impulsively, they often become the tipping point that pushes training into chronic fatigue.

With an understanding of how threshold, easy running, and high-intensity work fit together, we can now look at how to organize these elements into practical weekly training structures that work for real-world schedules.

# Applying Elite Principles to Real Life

# SIXTEEN

# Building a Week Around Your Schedule

Understanding how different types of training fit together is only useful if runners can actually apply it within their own schedules. Most people are not training twice per day, do not have unlimited recovery time, and are balancing running with work, family, and other responsibilities. For this reason, the Norwegian method must be adapted to fit realistic weekly routines, not idealized elite schedules.

The first step in building a sustainable training week is deciding how many days can realistically be devoted to running. This matters more than any single workout, because consistency over time is what drives long-term improvement. Whether a runner trains three days per week or six, the goal is to place higher-quality sessions where they can be performed well and surrounded by enough easy or rest days to allow recovery.

For runners training three to four days per week, the priority should be protecting one high-quality threshold session and one long aerobic run. These two workouts deliver the greatest return on investment for limited training time. The remaining runs should be easy and supportive, focused on building volume gradually and aiding recovery rather than chasing pace.

When training time is limited, the most effective threshold sessions are those that allow runners to accumulate a meaningful amount of work at controlled intensity without spiking fatigue. This is often done using intervals or steady blocks rather than one continuous hard effort.

A common and very effective format is three to four repeats of six to ten minutes at threshold effort, with short easy recovery between each repeat. For example, a runner might complete $4 \times$ 8 minutes at comfortably hard intensity with two minutes of easy jogging between efforts. This allows for strong aerobic stimulus while keeping pacing steady and repeatable.

Another option is a continuous steady run at threshold effort lasting twenty to thirty minutes. This format works well for runners who are comfortable holding pace and who recover well from sustained efforts, but it can be harder to pace correctly and easier to overdo, especially for newer runners.

Regardless of format, the goal is to finish the workout feeling worked but not depleted. Runners should feel confident they could repeat a similar session within a few days. If threshold sessions regularly leave runners overly sore or fatigued, the intensity or total duration is likely too high.

As fitness improves, progression comes from gradually extending total time spent at threshold, not from pushing harder. Increasing from twenty minutes to thirty or forty minutes of controlled work over several weeks builds endurance safely while maintaining consistency.

During these efforts, runners should be able to speak short phrases but not full sentences. A phrase like "I feel strong" or "almost there" should be possible, but holding a normal conversation would not be. Breathing should be deep and steady, not gasping or frantic, and form should remain controlled rather than strained. If runners are unable to speak at all or feel the need to slow dramatically before the final repeat, the effort is likely above threshold and should be adjusted down slightly.

In a four-day training week, a simple structure might look like this: a threshold session on Tuesday, an easy run on Wednesday, another easy run on Friday, and a long run on Sunday. This keeps demanding sessions separated by easier days and prevents fatigue from accumulating too quickly.

Runners training five to six days per week have more flexibility, but the same principles apply. Threshold sessions still need recovery on both sides, and easy days must remain truly easy. Instead of adding more intensity, extra training days are best used to increase low-intensity volume, which strengthens the aerobic system and improves durability.

In this type of schedule, most runners do well with one to two threshold sessions per week, one long run, and the remaining days devoted to easy running. High-intensity intervals or speed work can be added occasionally, but only when overall fatigue is low and threshold sessions are not being compromised.

Spacing between quality sessions is just as important as how many sessions are performed. Two demanding workouts placed back-to-back often reduce the effectiveness of both. Separating them with at least one easy day allows runners to approach each quality session with better energy, sharper pacing, and lower injury risk.

Long runs deserve special consideration within the weekly structure. Some long runs should remain entirely easy, especially during base training phases. At other times, controlled segments near threshold can be added to the middle or end of long runs, combining endurance and quality without creating an extra workout day.

This approach allows runners to accumulate meaningful training stress while keeping the total number of demanding days limited. Instead of stacking multiple hard workouts into the week, intensity is distributed in a way that supports recovery and consistency.

Another important factor in weekly planning is recognizing that not every week needs to look the same. Work schedules, travel, illness, and fatigue all influence what is realistic. Rather than forcing a rigid plan, runners benefit from having flexible templates that can be adjusted based on how the body is responding.

If a runner notices that threshold sessions are becoming harder to complete at a stable pace, or that easy days no longer feel restorative, it's usually a sign that weekly stress is too high. In these cases, reducing one quality session or shortening workouts is often more effective than trying to push through fatigue.

The goal of weekly structure is not to maximize suffering, but to create an environment where fitness can steadily build. When training fits into life instead of fighting against it, runners are far more likely to stay consistent, avoid injury, and continue improving over the long term.

In the next chapter, we'll focus on how to run threshold sessions at the right intensity without relying on lactate testing or expensive technology, using simple cues that any runner can apply.

# SEVENTEEN

# Running Threshold the Right Way Without Gadgets

One of the most common misconceptions about threshold training is that it requires laboratory testing, heart rate monitors, or handheld lactate meters to be done correctly. While these tools can be helpful in certain settings, they aren't necessary for most runners to train at the right intensity. In fact, many athletes learn to control threshold effort more accurately by paying attention to internal cues rather than external numbers.

Threshold effort is best understood as the highest intensity that can be sustained steadily without rapidly accumulating fatigue. At this effort level, breathing is deep and rhythmic, muscles are working, and focus is required, but the pace still feels controlled rather than frantic. The goal is to work hard enough to stimulate aerobic adaptation without tipping into a level of effort that can only be maintained for a few minutes.

From a practical standpoint, threshold should feel "comfortably hard." A useful test is conversation. At threshold, runners shouldn't be able to hold a normal conversation, but they should be able to speak short phrases if needed. A simple rule is this: you should be able to say, "I feel strong and in control," but you should not be able to say something much longer, like, "I could keep chatting while running like this forever." If full sentences come easily, the effort is probably too easy. If even short phrases are difficult or broken, the intensity is likely too high and should be backed off slightly.

Breathing provides another reliable cue. During threshold efforts, breathing should be strong and purposeful but not panicked. Inhalations and exhalations fall into a steady rhythm that can be maintained for extended periods. If breathing becomes irregular or gasping, it's a sign that effort has crossed into higher-intensity territory.

Pacing consistency is also critical. A well-executed threshold session should feel similar from the first repeat to the last. Small increases in fatigue are expected, but pace should not drop sharply and form should remain controlled. If speed deteriorates significantly, intensity was likely set too aggressively at the start.

Another helpful guideline is that threshold workouts should feel demanding but repeatable. Runners should finish sessions feeling challenged yet confident they could perform a similar workout again within a few days. When workouts consistently leave runners exhausted or sore for multiple days, intensity or volume is too high.

It's also important to recognize that threshold pace changes over time and can vary based on conditions. Heat, hills, fatigue, and life stress all influence how the body responds to training.

Rather than chasing exact paces, runners are better served by adjusting effort to match how the body feels on a given day while staying within the same general intensity range.

For runners who prefer some external guidance, recent race performances can provide useful benchmarks, but they should reflect current fitness, not results from many months ago. Threshold pace is typically about 20 to 40 seconds per mile (12 to 25 seconds per kilometer) slower than current 5K race pace, usually close to recent 10K pace, and slightly faster than half-marathon pace. This roughly matches the fastest speed that could be held for about 45 to 60 minutes. These are only approximations, and effort cues should always take priority over rigid pace targets.

One of the most common mistakes with threshold training is turning sessions into unofficial races. This often happens when runners feel good and gradually push beyond the intended intensity. While occasional harder efforts are not harmful, consistently exceeding threshold turns these sessions into high-intensity workouts, increasing recovery demands and reducing the ability to train frequently.

Controlled intensity is what allows threshold training to be repeated week after week. It's better to slightly under-shoot the ideal effort than to push too hard and compromise consistency. Over time, as fitness improves, the same controlled effort will naturally produce faster paces.

For runners new to threshold training, it can take several weeks to develop a good feel for the right intensity. Early sessions may feel awkward or slower than expected, but learning to stay relaxed while working hard is a skill that improves with practice. Patience during this phase pays off with more sustainable progress later.

Ultimately, threshold training without gadgets relies on awareness, discipline, and consistency. By learning to recognize the effort that is challenging but controlled, runners can apply the core principles of the Norwegian method without specialized equipment or laboratory testing.

In the next chapter, we'll look at how lactate testing can be used to fine-tune intensity for runners who have access to it, and when this extra level of precision is most useful.

# EIGHTEEN

# Using Lactate to Fine-Tune Intensity (Optional)

Lactate is most commonly measured using a small handheld device similar to a blood glucose meter. A tiny drop of blood is taken from the fingertip or earlobe using a sterile lancet, placed on a test strip, and analyzed by the device within seconds. The result is displayed as a number measured in millimoles per liter, often written as mmol/L. The prick is very small and feels like a quick pinprick, and testing can be done directly at the track or training venue during workouts.

Testing is usually performed during structured interval sessions rather than during normal easy runs. An athlete completes a repeat at a set pace, then pauses briefly while a coach takes a small blood sample. If lactate remains stable across repeats, the pace is likely close to true threshold. If lactate rises quickly, the pace is adjusted downward. This allows intensity to be fine-tuned so that sessions remain aerobic rather than drifting into higher-intensity territory.

There are other ways people attempt to estimate threshold, but none directly measure lactate. Some runners use heart rate as a rough guide, often targeting a certain percentage of maximum heart rate. While heart rate can be useful for tracking general effort, it's influenced by many factors, including heat, fatigue, hydration, caffeine, stress, and sleep. It also tends to drift upward during longer efforts even when pace remains steady, which can make it difficult to use as a precise control tool during threshold workouts.

Because of this, heart rate is best used as supporting information rather than as the primary way to set intensity. If pace, breathing, and effort feel controlled but heart rate is slightly higher than expected on a hot or stressful day, it doesn't necessarily mean intensity is wrong. Likewise, a low heart rate doesn't guarantee that pacing is appropriate if the runner is pushing too hard mechanically or struggling to recover between sessions.

When runners do use pace or heart rate as reference points, accuracy improves when testing and training are done under consistent, controlled conditions. Flat routes or track ovals reduce the effects of hills on effort, while moderate temperatures limit heat-related heart rate drift. Being well hydrated, adequately fueled, and reasonably rested also makes pacing data more reliable. Trying to judge threshold after poor sleep, during extreme heat, or at the end of a stressful week will almost always distort the data.

For this reason, recent race results or well-paced time trials on flat courses provide the most useful external benchmarks. Comparing how a given pace feels across similar conditions gives far better feedback than relying on isolated workouts run under very different circumstances. Over time, patterns in effort, pace, and recovery provide clearer guidance than any single data point.

Lab-based testing is another option, where athletes run on treadmills or bikes while lactate and breathing data are collected at increasing intensities. These tests can provide detailed performance profiles, but they are expensive and not practical for frequent feedback during normal training. Some wearable devices also claim to estimate lactate or metabolic thresholds using algorithms, but these don't actually measure lactate and should be treated as optional refinement tools, not a requirement.

Because of these limitations, most runners are better served by using effort cues, pacing consistency, breathing patterns, and recovery quality to guide threshold training. Lactate testing becomes most useful when training volumes are very high, performance goals are highly specific, or an athlete is working closely with a coach who can interpret the data and adjust training accordingly. For everyone else, lactate testing is an optional refinement tool, not a requirement for successful threshold training.

In the next chapter, we'll look at how to structure threshold sessions across the week and over longer training blocks, including how to progress volume safely and adjust intensity as race day approaches.

# NINETEEN

# Structuring Threshold Sessions and Progressing Over Time

Once runners understand how to control threshold intensity, the next step is learning how to structure these sessions across weeks and months. Progress doesn't come from pushing harder each workout, but from gradually increasing the amount of productive work the body can absorb while staying within recoverable limits.

The most reliable way to progress threshold training is by increasing total time spent at threshold, not by increasing intensity. Running faster than threshold quickly turns sessions into high-intensity workouts that require longer recovery and reduce how often quality training can be repeated. By contrast, adding small amounts of controlled work builds aerobic capacity steadily while preserving consistency.

For most runners, a good starting point is around twenty minutes of total threshold work in a session, whether done continuously or broken into intervals. Over several weeks, this can gradually increase toward thirty or even forty minutes of total threshold time. These increases should be modest and spaced out, allowing the body time to adapt before additional workload is added.

Progression can take several forms. Runners might add another repeat, slightly extend the duration of each interval, or increase the length of continuous threshold efforts. What matters is that only one variable changes at a time, and that changes are small enough to maintain stable pacing and good recovery.

Adding more threshold sessions per week should come only after current sessions feel manageable and recovery remains strong. Many runners progress best by first extending the length of a single threshold workout before introducing a second weekly session. This ensures the aerobic system is developing before overall training stress is increased.

When two threshold sessions are included in the week, spacing becomes even more important. These sessions should be separated by at least one, and ideally two, easy days. Long runs and strength training should also be considered when planning the week, as accumulated fatigue from other activities can affect the quality of threshold sessions.

Training is rarely linear, and not every week should push volume higher. Periodic lighter weeks help absorb adaptations and reduce injury risk. For most runners, this means scheduling a lighter or "down" week after about three to five weeks of gradually increasing workload. During these weeks, threshold volume may be reduced by 30 to 50 percent, sessions may be shortened, or one quality workout may be replaced with easier aerobic running. Mileage can also be slightly lower, and overall intensity should feel more manageable.

These lighter weeks are not a step backward. They allow fatigue to drop while fitness continues to consolidate, often leaving runners feeling stronger and fresher when normal training resumes. Many athletes notice that workouts feel easier and pacing becomes more stable in the weeks following a recovery period, even without increasing training stress.

The exact timing doesn't need to be rigid. If training feels strong and recovery is excellent, a runner may extend a block slightly longer. If fatigue, soreness, or motivation begin to dip earlier than expected, it's often wise to insert a lighter week sooner rather than pushing through. Letting the body catch up before problems appear is far more effective than trying to recover after performance has already declined.

This ebb and flow of training stress is a key feature of sustainable long-term improvement. It also makes it easier to recognize when progression may be happening too quickly. If pacing becomes inconsistent, recovery takes longer than usual, or motivation drops, these are often signals that workload should be reduced temporarily. Backing off for a short period often leads to stronger training in the following weeks.

Seasonal goals should also influence how threshold training is structured. During base-building phases, threshold may appear less frequently while overall aerobic volume increases. As race preparation approaches, threshold becomes more prominent, helping sharpen race-specific endurance without relying heavily on high-intensity sessions.

Rather than chasing constant improvement from week to week, runners benefit from thinking in terms of training blocks. Each block focuses on building a specific capacity, followed by a short period of consolidation before the next phase begins. This approach allows fitness to build in layers rather than through constant strain.

In practical terms, a training block typically lasts between six and ten weeks, including both the gradual build-up and a lighter recovery period. Over the course of a year, most recreational runners can realistically complete three to five focused training blocks, depending on race schedules, life demands, and recovery needs. Each block doesn't need to chase peak fitness, but should aim to slightly raise the runner's overall baseline before the next cycle begins.

Some blocks may emphasize general aerobic development, others may focus more on threshold endurance, and later blocks may sharpen race-specific fitness. Between these phases, short periods of reduced training help absorb gains and reset fatigue before the next progression begins. This long-term rhythm is far more effective than trying to push hard every month of the year.

Viewing training this way also reduces pressure to improve constantly. Not every block will produce dramatic breakthroughs, and that's normal. What matters is that fitness trends upward across the year, even if individual weeks or races don't always reflect immediate progress.

Ultimately, effective progression is about patience and restraint. Threshold training works best when it can be repeated consistently over long periods, not when it's pushed to extremes for short bursts. By increasing workload gradually and respecting recovery, runners create the conditions for sustainable performance gains.

In the next chapter, we'll look at how threshold training should be adjusted based on race distance, and how preparation differs for 5K, 10K, and half-marathon goals.

PART V

# Race-Specific Preparation and Training Plans

# TWENTY

# Choosing the Right Plan for Your Experience Level

Before selecting a specific training schedule, it's important to choose a structure that matches current fitness, training history, and available time. The most effective plan is not the most aggressive one, but the one that can be followed consistently while allowing proper recovery between harder sessions.

Experience level matters more than current race pace. A runner who has only been training consistently for a few months will respond very differently to workload than someone who has been running for several years, even if their current race times are similar. Adaptation depends not just on cardiovascular fitness, but also on how well muscles, tendons, and joints tolerate repeated stress.

For this reason, the plans in this book are organized primarily by how many days per week a runner can train and how much quality work can be handled without compromising recovery. Rather than forcing runners into strict pace categories, the focus is on choosing a structure that supports steady improvement over time.

Runners should generally begin with the lowest training frequency that fits their schedule and comfort level, then move to higher-volume options only after several weeks of stable training. Progressing too quickly often leads to fatigue, stalled workouts, or injury, which ultimately slows long-term development.

Three and four-day-per-week plans are well suited for runners who are newer to structured training, returning after time away, balancing running with demanding schedules, or combining running with other sports or gym-based training. These plans focus on one key threshold session and one long aerobic run each week, supported by easy runs that build aerobic capacity while promoting recovery.

This structure delivers strong fitness gains with relatively low injury risk, and it also provides flexibility. If a session must be missed due to work, travel, or fatigue, the overall rhythm of the week can usually be maintained without disrupting progression.

Five and six-day-per-week plans are more appropriate for runners who already tolerate regular mileage and recover well between sessions. These plans include more easy running, which strengthens the aerobic base and improves durability. The extra days are not intended to add more hard workouts, but to distribute aerobic training more evenly across the week.

With higher-frequency training, threshold sessions and long runs can often be performed with better energy and more stable pacing because fatigue is spread across more days rather than concentrated into fewer sessions. However, runners should already be comfortable completing quality workouts without lingering soreness or persistent fatigue before moving to these plans.

Race goals also influence plan selection. Runners preparing for shorter events such as the 5K may include slightly more frequent quality work and occasional speed-focused sessions, while those training for longer races like the half marathon typically require more aerobic volume and longer sustained efforts. Even so, the overall structure remains similar, with threshold training forming the backbone of weekly quality work and easy mileage supporting recovery and endurance.

No plan should be treated as rigid. Missed workouts, stressful weeks, and unexpected fatigue are part of real-world training. When this happens, runners should prioritize the most important sessions, usually the threshold workout and the long run, and allow easy runs to be shortened or skipped if necessary.

If fatigue begins to accumulate or workouts start to feel consistently harder than expected, it's better to repeat a week of training rather than pushing forward. Fitness improves when training stress is absorbed, not simply when workouts are completed on schedule.

Many runners benefit from staying within the same general plan structure for several months before moving to higher volumes or more frequent training. Jumping between plans too often can disrupt adaptation and increase injury risk. A simple approach is to complete one or two full training blocks within a given plan level before considering a step up.

Choosing the right plan is about creating an environment where training can be repeated week after week without constant setbacks. When structure, recovery, and life demands are aligned, improvement becomes far more predictable and sustainable.

In the next chapter, we'll look at how to read the training plans, how to interpret effort descriptions, and how to adjust sessions when conditions or recovery levels change.

# TWENTY-ONE

# How to Read and Adjust the Training Plans

Training plans are meant to guide decision-making, not to be followed blindly. Even the best-designed schedule cannot account for daily variations in sleep, stress, work demands, illness, or unexpected life events. Learning how to interpret and adjust a plan is just as important as choosing the right one.

Each training week in this book is built around a small number of key sessions, usually a threshold workout and a long run, supported by easy aerobic runs. These key sessions provide the strongest stimulus for improvement and should be prioritized whenever possible. If time or energy is limited during a given week, it's better to protect these sessions and reduce or shorten easy runs rather than forcing every workout onto the schedule.

Effort descriptions in the plans are intentionally written in broad terms such as easy, steady, threshold, or hard. These labels refer to how the running should feel, not just to pace on a watch. On days labeled easy, runners should be able to breathe comfortably and hold full conversations. On threshold days, breathing should be deep and controlled, and short phrases should still be possible, but full conversations should not. Pace may vary slightly from day to day depending on conditions and fatigue, and that's normal.

Weather, terrain, and daily stress can all affect how fast a given effort feels. On hot or humid days, heart rate will often be higher at the same pace, and perceived effort may rise even if speed remains unchanged. On days following poor sleep or hard workouts, legs may feel heavy even at normal training speeds. In these situations, adjusting pace to match the intended effort is far more productive than forcing a predetermined number on the watch.

If a threshold workout feels unusually difficult early in the session, runners should not hesitate to shorten intervals, extend recovery, or reduce total volume for that day. Completing slightly less work at proper intensity is more beneficial than struggling through a session that drifts into higher intensity and compromises recovery for the rest of the week.

Missed workouts are inevitable over the course of a training cycle. When this happens, runners should resist the urge to cram sessions into later days to make up for what was missed. Stacking hard workouts too closely together often reduces the quality of both and increases injury risk. It's usually better to resume the normal schedule and allow the training rhythm to reestablish itself.

When fatigue accumulates across several days or weeks, the solution is not always to push harder. Signs such as declining pacing, persistent soreness, disrupted sleep, or loss of motivation often indicate that recovery is falling behind training stress. In these cases, reducing volume for a few days or replacing a quality session with easy running can restore training momentum more effectively than forcing additional work.

Runners should also view plans as flexible templates rather than rigid prescriptions. If a particular week is especially busy, shortening runs or shifting sessions by a day can help maintain consistency without increasing stress. The overall pattern of training matters far more than the exact placement of any single workout.

Long-term progress depends on staying healthy and motivated. A plan that feels sustainable encourages consistency, while one that feels overwhelming often leads to burnout or injury. Adjusting training to match current capacity is not a sign of weakness, but a skill that improves results over time.

As runners gain experience, they will become better at recognizing how their bodies respond to different workloads and conditions. This awareness allows training to become more individualized, even when following a structured plan.

In the next chapters, we'll apply these principles to specific race distances and show how threshold training, easy running, and long runs are balanced differently for the 5K, 10K, and half marathon, along with example weekly structures for each.

# TWENTY-TWO

# Training for the 5K Using Norwegian Principles

Although the 5K is considered a short race, it's still heavily dependent on aerobic fitness. For most runners, well over eighty percent of the energy used during a 5K comes from the aerobic system. This is why threshold training plays such an important role in 5K preparation, even for athletes who think of the event as primarily speed-based.

The Norwegian approach to 5K training focuses on building strong aerobic endurance through frequent, controlled threshold work, supported by easy mileage and occasional high-intensity sessions. Instead of relying on repeated all-out interval workouts, fitness is built through consistent efforts that can be repeated week after week without excessive fatigue.

Most 5K training weeks should include at least one threshold session, one long aerobic run, and several easy runs. Runners training more frequently may benefit from a second controlled threshold session. The exact number of sessions depends on training frequency and experience level, but threshold remains the primary quality stimulus throughout most of the training cycle.

Threshold sessions for 5K runners are often performed using interval formats that allow runners to accumulate meaningful time at controlled intensity. Examples include four to five repeats of five to eight minutes, or longer sets such as three repeats of ten minutes, with short easy recoveries between efforts (60–120 seconds of easy jogging). These sessions improve the ability to sustain fast aerobic paces without accumulating excessive fatigue.

While threshold training builds the engine, speed and aerobic power still need to be addressed, especially as races approach. This is where sessions such as short intervals, hill work, or formats like the 4×4 method can be included strategically. These workouts help raise the ceiling of aerobic capacity and sharpen the ability to run fast without turning every week into a battle for recovery.

For most runners, high-intensity sessions should appear no more than once per week, and often less frequently during heavy threshold phases. These workouts are best placed on weeks where overall fatigue is low and recovery between sessions is strong. When used correctly, they complement threshold training rather than compete with it.

Easy running remains essential throughout 5K training. Easy days allow the body to absorb harder sessions, build aerobic volume, and maintain durability. Without enough easy mileage, even well-designed threshold programs can become unsustainable.

Long runs play an important supporting role, even for shorter races like the 5K. While the race itself is short, long runs improve overall endurance, strengthen connective tissue, and enhance recovery capacity. Most 5K runners benefit from weekly long runs lasting roughly 45 to 75 minutes, performed at relaxed aerobic intensity.

Most recreational runners run between 15 and 45 miles per week (25–72 km), depending on experience, goals, and available training time. Runners at the lower end of this range can still make strong progress when threshold sessions and long runs are placed consistently and recovery is well managed.

Higher mileage does not automatically mean better results. Many runners improve more from consistent moderate volume with well-placed threshold sessions than from chasing high weekly totals they cannot recover from.

As race day approaches, training gradually becomes more specific. Threshold sessions may shift slightly closer to race pace, high-intensity work may become more targeted, and overall volume may decrease modestly to reduce fatigue. However, the core structure of controlled aerobic training remains in place, preventing fitness from being replaced by short-term sharpness alone.

Rather than drastically changing training in the final weeks, the Norwegian method emphasizes refining what has already been built. Small adjustments in intensity and volume allow runners to arrive at race day fresh while preserving the aerobic foundation developed over months of consistent training.

Use your most recent 5K result from the past six to eight weeks when referencing this table. These ranges are intended as guidelines, not strict rules. On hot days, hilly routes, or during periods of accumulated fatigue, paces may need to be slightly slower to maintain the correct effort level. Effort and breathing cues should always take priority over exact numbers on a watch.

## 5K Training Pace Guide (Based on Recent 5K Time)

| 5K Time | 5K Pace | Threshold Pace | Easy Run Pace |
| --- | --- | --- | --- |
| 15:00 | 4:49/mi (3:00/km) | 5:10–5:25/mi (3:12–3:22/km) | 6:10–7:00/mi (3:50–4:20/km) |
| 17:30 | 5:38/mi (3:30/km) | 6:00–6:15/mi (3:44–3:54/km) | 7:00–8:00/mi (4:20–5:00/km) |
| 20:00 | 6:26/mi (4:00/km) | 6:50–7:05/mi (4:15–4:25/km) | 8:00–9:00/mi (5:00–5:35/km) |
| 22:30 | 7:14/mi (4:30/km) | 7:40–8:00/mi (4:45–5:00/km) | 9:00–10:00/mi (5:35–6:10/km) |
| 25:00 | 8:03/mi (5:00/km) | 8:30–8:55/mi (5:15–5:30/km) | 10:00–11:00/mi (6:10–6:50/km) |
| 30:00 | 9:39/mi (6:00/km) | 10:10–10:35/mi (6:20–6:35/km) | 12:00–13:00/mi (7:30–8:05/km) |
| 35:00 | 11:16/mi (7:00/km) | 11:45–12:15/mi (7:18–7:38/km) | 13:30–15:00/mi (8:25–9:20/km) |
| 40:00 | 12:52/mi (8:00/km) | 13:30–14:15/mi (8:24–8:50/km) | 15:30–17:00/mi (9:40–10:35/km) |

The table on the next page shows how these principles can be arranged across different weekly training frequencies. Regardless of how many days are available, threshold and long runs remain the anchors of the week, while easy days protect recovery and consistency.

Runners training five or six days per week may include two threshold sessions, separated by easy days, along with a long run and occasional high-intensity or hill sessions placed carefully to avoid interfering with recovery.

The exact placement of workouts is less important than maintaining proper spacing between demanding sessions and ensuring easy days remain truly easy.

## Example Weekly Structure for 5K Preparation (Norwegian-Inspired)

| Day | 3 Days / Week | 4 Days / Week | 5 Days / Week | 6 Days / Week |
| --- | --- | --- | --- | --- |
| Mon | Rest / Cross-Train | Rest / Cross-Train | Easy Run | Easy Run |
| Tue | Threshold Session | Threshold Session | Threshold Session | Threshold Session |
| Wed | Rest | Easy Run | Easy Run | Easy Run |
| Thu | Easy Run | Rest | Speed / Hills or Short Intervals | Speed / Hills or Short Intervals |
| Fri | Rest | Easy Run or Strides | Rest or Easy Run | Easy Run |
| Sat | Rest | Rest | Easy Run | Easy Run |
| Sun | Long Run (Easy) | Long Run (Easy) | Long Run (Easy) | Long Run (Easy) |

When the plan lists "rest or cross-training," this refers to low-impact aerobic exercise that supports cardiovascular fitness without the pounding of running. Activities such as cycling, swimming, rowing, or using an elliptical trainer can increase aerobic volume while reducing stress on the joints and muscles. These sessions should remain easy and comfortable, similar in effort to an easy run, and are intended to support recovery rather than replace key running workouts.

Cross-training is optional, but it can be especially useful for runners who are increasing training frequency, managing minor aches, or balancing running with strength training or other sports. When used appropriately, it allows runners to build fitness while protecting long-term durability.

When the plan lists "speed / hills or short intervals," this refers to brief, higher-intensity work that improves leg turnover, running economy, and top-end aerobic power for the 5K. These sessions should feel fast but controlled, with smooth form and consistent pacing rather than all-out sprinting. Keep the total volume modest and stop the workout while you still feel sharp. This workout is optional and is best added only if your threshold session and long run are already feeling stable week to week.

When the plan lists "easy run or strides," strides are short accelerations added to the end of an easy run to keep your mechanics snappy. A typical strides set is 4 to 8 repeats of 15 to 25 seconds at a fast but relaxed pace, with full easy recovery between each one. You should finish feeling lighter and more coordinated, not out of breath or sore. If strides start to feel like a workout, they've gone too hard.

In the next chapter, we'll look at how training priorities shift slightly for the 10K, where sustained aerobic strength becomes even more central to performance.

# TWENTY-THREE

# Training for the 10K Using Norwegian Principles

The 10K sits in a unique position between speed and endurance. While it's still raced at relatively high intensity, it's even more dependent on aerobic fitness than the 5K. For most runners, well over ninety percent of the energy used during a 10K comes from the aerobic system. This means that the ability to sustain strong aerobic effort for extended periods becomes the primary limiter of performance.

Because of this, threshold training becomes even more central to 10K preparation. The Norwegian approach emphasizes developing the capacity to run comfortably hard for longer stretches of time, rather than relying heavily on short, maximal efforts. Instead of repeatedly practicing extreme intensity, fitness is built through frequent, controlled aerobic stress that can be repeated consistently across the training cycle.

Most 10K training weeks are built around one or two threshold sessions, one long aerobic run, and several easy runs. Compared to 5K training, threshold sessions for 10K runners tend to be slightly longer and more continuous, reflecting the sustained nature of the race itself. The goal is not just to reach threshold, but to remain there comfortably for extended durations.

Threshold sessions for 10K preparation often use longer intervals or steady efforts that accumulate thirty to forty minutes of total work at threshold intensity. Examples include three to four repeats of eight to twelve minutes with short recoveries (60 to 120 seconds of easy jogging), or continuous threshold runs lasting twenty-five to thirty-five minutes. These formats improve the ability to maintain fast aerobic pace without significant lactate buildup or large fluctuations in effort.

Progression for 10K runners typically comes from extending time at threshold rather than increasing intensity. Over several weeks, runners may gradually lengthen intervals, reduce recovery time slightly, or extend steady threshold segments. These changes should remain subtle, allowing pacing to stay smooth and recovery between sessions to remain reliable.

While threshold work forms the backbone of training, occasional higher-intensity sessions still have a place, especially as race day approaches. Shorter intervals, controlled hill sessions, or formats such as the 4×4 method can help improve aerobic power and sharpen leg speed. However, these sessions should be used strategically and sparingly, usually no more than once per week and often less frequently during heavy threshold phases.

Easy running continues to play a critical role in 10K training. Easy days support recovery, increase aerobic volume, and allow threshold sessions to be performed with higher quality.

Without enough low-intensity mileage, threshold work becomes harder to absorb and consistency begins to suffer.

Long runs also become more influential as race distance increases. For 10K runners, long runs build durability, strengthen connective tissue, and improve the ability to sustain moderate efforts late into races. Most runners benefit from completing one long run each week lasting roughly sixty to ninety minutes at a relaxed aerobic pace. The majority of this run should feel comfortable and conversational, with breathing under control and no sense of strain. During certain phases of training, usually when preparing more specifically for an upcoming race, short steady or moderate segments can be added within the long run to gently increase fatigue resistance. These faster sections should remain controlled and make up only a small portion of the total run, such as a slightly quicker final ten to twenty minutes or a few short pickups spaced throughout the session. The purpose of these additions is not to turn the long run into a hard workout, but to introduce small amounts of sustained effort while preserving the overall easy nature of the run.

For 10K preparation, most recreational runners fall somewhere between 25 and 60 miles per week (40–95 km). Higher volumes can be beneficial, but only when intensity is well controlled and recovery remains strong.

As competition approaches, training gradually becomes more race-specific. Threshold sessions may drift slightly closer to 10K pace, and occasional race-pace intervals may be introduced to improve pacing familiarity and confidence. Overall training volume may also be reduced modestly, typically by about 15 to 30 percent, to allow fatigue to drop while preserving fitness. Quality sessions are usually maintained, while easy mileage is reduced slightly.

Rather than making drastic changes late in the cycle, the Norwegian method favors refining existing fitness through controlled adjustments. This helps prevent the common mistake of replacing aerobic strength with short-term sharpness that fades quickly under race conditions.

The paces on the table on the next page are most useful for guiding threshold sessions and steady aerobic segments. Easy runs should remain relaxed even if pace falls slower than the listed ranges.

## 10K Training Pace Guide (Based on Recent 10K Time)

| 10K Time | 10K Pace | Threshold Pace | Easy Run Pace |
| --- | --- | --- | --- |
| 30:00 | 4:49/mi (3:00/km) | 5:05–5:20/mi (3:10–3:20/km) | 6:00–6:50/mi (3:45–4:15/km) |
| 35:00 | 5:38/mi (3:30/km) | 6:00–6:15/mi (3:44–3:54/km) | 7:00–8:00/mi (4:20–5:00/km) |
| 40:00 | 6:26/mi (4:00/km) | 6:50–7:05/mi (4:15–4:25/km) | 8:00–9:00/mi (5:00–5:35/km) |
| 45:00 | 7:14/mi (4:30/km) | 7:40–8:00/mi (4:45–5:00/km) | 9:00–10:00/mi (5:35–6:10/km) |
| 50:00 | 8:03/mi (5:00/km) | 8:30–8:55/mi (5:15–5:30/km) | 10:00–11:00/mi (6:10–6:50/km) |
| 55:00 | 8:51/mi (5:30/km) | 9:20–9:45/mi (5:50–6:05/km) | 11:00–12:00/mi (6:50–7:30/km) |
| 60:00 | 9:39/mi (6:00/km) | 10:10–10:35/mi (6:20–6:35/km) | 12:00–13:00/mi (7:30–8:05/km) |
| 70:00 | 11:16/mi (7:00/km) | 11:45–12:15/mi (7:18–7:38/km) | 13:30–15:00/mi (8:25–9:20/km) |
| 80:00 | 12:52/mi (8:00/km) | 13:30–14:15/mi (8:24–8:50/km) | 15:30–17:00/mi (9:40–10:35/km) |

Regardless of how many days are available, threshold and long runs remain the anchors of the week, while easy days protect recovery and consistency.

Runners training five days per week may include two threshold-focused sessions, separated by easy days, along with one long run and two easy runs. Occasional short speed or hill sessions can be added during specific phases, but only if recovery remains strong.

Runners training six days per week generally benefit from maintaining two quality sessions, one focused on threshold and another that may include hills or short intervals depending on the phase of training. All remaining days should remain easy, with the long run kept as a weekly anchor.

Regardless of frequency, quality sessions should always be separated by at least one easy day, and easy days should remain truly easy. When fatigue accumulates, reducing intensity is usually more effective than reducing overall consistency.

**Example Weekly Structure for 10K Preparation (Norwegian-Inspired)**

| Day | 3 Days / Week | 4 Days / Week | 5 Days / Week | 6 Days / Week |
| --- | --- | --- | --- | --- |
| Mon | Rest / Cross-Train | Rest / Cross-Train | Easy Run | Easy Run |
| Tue | Threshold Session | Threshold Session | Threshold Session | Threshold Session |
| Wed | Rest | Easy Run | Easy Run | Easy Run |
| Thu | Easy Run | Rest | Easy Run or Strides | Speed / Hills or Short Intervals |
| Fri | Rest | Easy Run | Rest or Easy Run | Easy Run |
| Sat | Rest | Rest | Easy Run | Easy Run |
| Sun | Long Run (Easy) | Long Run (Easy) | Long Run (Easy) | Long Run (Easy) |

## How 10K Training Differs From 5K Training

While both distances rely heavily on aerobic fitness, 10K training shifts slightly toward longer sustained efforts and greater emphasis on endurance. Threshold sessions become longer, recovery between repeats may be slightly shorter, and long runs become more influential in overall performance.

High-intensity sessions tend to play a smaller role compared to 5K preparation. Speed is still relevant, but it is rarely the primary limiter in the 10K. Most improvements come from increasing the ability to hold strong aerobic pace rather than from increasing peak speed.

This does not mean that speed work disappears entirely, but it becomes more about maintaining efficiency and coordination than about pushing maximum intensity. Short strides and occasional hills are usually sufficient to support mechanics without adding unnecessary fatigue.

Ultimately, successful 10K preparation is built on consistency, controlled intensity, and steady progression. When runners can repeat quality threshold sessions week after week while remaining healthy and motivated, performance tends to improve naturally without requiring extreme workouts.

In the next chapter, we'll shift focus to the half marathon, where aerobic endurance becomes even more dominant and long-run structure plays a larger role in overall training design.

# TWENTY-FOUR

# Training for the Half Marathon Using Norwegian Principles

The half marathon is where aerobic endurance becomes the dominant factor in performance. While speed and running economy still matter, success in this race depends primarily on how well a runner can sustain strong aerobic effort for a long period of time without accumulating excessive fatigue. This makes threshold training and steady aerobic work even more important than in shorter races.

In the Norwegian approach, half marathon preparation is built around developing the ability to run comfortably hard for extended durations while maintaining efficient movement and stable pacing. Rather than relying heavily on short, intense workouts, training focuses on repeated exposure to controlled aerobic stress that strengthens the body's ability to process fatigue and maintain form late into the race.

Most half marathon training weeks are anchored by one or two threshold-focused sessions, one long run, and several easy runs. Compared to 5K and 10K training, threshold sessions for the half marathon tend to be longer and more continuous, reflecting the sustained effort required on race day.

Threshold workouts for half marathon preparation often accumulate thirty-five to fifty minutes of total work at threshold intensity. Examples include three repeats of twelve to fifteen minutes with short recoveries (60 to 120 seconds of easy jogging), or continuous steady efforts lasting twenty-five to forty minutes. These sessions improve the ability to sustain strong aerobic pace while remaining metabolically controlled.

In addition to threshold training, steady aerobic running just below threshold becomes increasingly valuable. These efforts are slightly easier than threshold but still faster than normal easy pace and can be sustained for longer periods. Steady runs help build fatigue resistance and improve the ability to maintain form and pace when tired, which is critical in the later stages of a half marathon.

While higher-intensity workouts can still appear occasionally, they play a much smaller role in half marathon training compared to shorter races. Short intervals and hill work may be used sparingly to maintain running mechanics and aerobic power, but they are not the primary drivers of performance at this distance.

Easy running continues to form the foundation of the training week. Easy days support recovery, increase aerobic volume, and allow quality sessions to be performed consistently. Without sufficient easy mileage, threshold and steady sessions become harder to absorb, and overall training rhythm begins to suffer.

Long runs take on even greater importance during half marathon preparation. These runs build muscular endurance, improve fuel utilization, and strengthen connective tissues. Most runners benefit from weekly long runs lasting roughly 90–130 minutes, performed mostly at relaxed aerobic pace. During later preparation phases, short steady segments may be added to the middle or end of long runs to improve fatigue resistance without turning the session into a full race simulation.

For half marathon training, recent 10K performances provide the most reliable reference for setting training paces, as they reflect sustained aerobic fitness more accurately than shorter races.

**Half Marathon Training Pace Guide (Based on Recent 10K Time)**

| 10K Time | 10K Pace | Threshold Pace | Steady Aerobic Pace | Easy Run Pace |
|---|---|---|---|---|
| 30:00 | 4:49/mi (3:00/km) | 5:05–5:20/mi (3:10–3:20/km) | 5:30–5:50/mi (3:25–3:38/km) | 6:10–7:00/mi (3:50–4:20/km) |
| 35:00 | 5:38/mi (3:30/km) | 6:00–6:15/mi (3:44–3:54/km) | 6:30–6:50/mi (4:02–4:15/km) | 7:00–8:00/mi (4:20–5:00/km) |
| 40:00 | 6:26/mi (4:00/km) | 6:50–7:05/mi (4:15–4:25/km) | 7:15–7:40/mi (4:30–4:45/km) | 8:00–9:00/mi (5:00–5:35/km) |
| 45:00 | 7:14/mi (4:30/km) | 7:40–8:00/mi (4:45–5:00/km) | 8:10–8:40/mi (5:05–5:25/km) | 9:00–10:00/mi (5:35–6:10/km) |
| 50:00 | 8:03/mi (5:00/km) | 8:30–8:55/mi (5:15–5:30/km) | 9:00–9:40/mi (5:35–6:00/km) | 10:00–11:00/mi (6:10–6:50/km) |
| 55:00 | 8:51/mi (5:30/km) | 9:20–9:45/mi (5:50–6:05/km) | 10:00–10:40/mi (6:10–6:40/km) | 11:00–12:00/mi (6:50–7:30/km) |
| 60:00 | 9:39/mi (6:00/km) | 10:10–10:35/mi (6:20–6:35/km) | 10:50–11:30/mi (6:45–7:10/km) | 12:00–13:00/mi (7:30–8:05/km) |
| 70:00 | 11:16/mi (7:00/km) | 11:45–12:15/mi (7:18–7:38/km) | 12:30–13:20/mi (7:45–8:15/km) | 13:30–15:00/mi (8:25–9:20/km) |
| 80:00 | 12:52/mi (8:00/km) | 13:30–14:15/mi (8:24–8:50/km) | 14:20–15:30/mi (8:55–9:40/km) | 15:30–17:00/mi (9:40–10:35/km) |

Use your most recent 10K result from the past six to eight weeks when referencing this table. These ranges are intended as guidelines, not strict rules. On hot days, hilly routes, or during periods of accumulated fatigue, paces may need to be slightly slower to maintain the correct effort level. Effort and breathing cues should always take priority over exact numbers on a watch.

For half marathon training, most recreational runners typically fall between 30-70 miles per week (50–110 km), depending on experience, goals, and recovery capacity. Higher volumes can support performance, but only when intensity is carefully controlled and easy days remain truly easy.

As race day approaches, training gradually becomes more specific to half marathon demands. Threshold sessions may shift slightly closer to race pace, steady runs may become more prominent, and long runs may include controlled pace segments. Overall weekly volume is usually reduced modestly, typically by about 15-30%, to allow fatigue to drop while preserving fitness. Quality sessions are maintained, while easy mileage is reduced slightly.

Rather than introducing drastic new workouts late in the cycle, the Norwegian method focuses on refining existing fitness. This approach helps runners arrive at the start line feeling strong and fresh rather than tired from last-minute intensity.

The table below shows how these principles can be arranged across different weekly training frequencies. Regardless of how many days are available, threshold and long runs remain the anchors of the week, while easy days protect recovery and consistency.

**Example Weekly Structure for Half Marathon Preparation (Norwegian-Inspired)**

| Day | 3 Days / Week | 4 Days / Week | 5 Days / Week | 6 Days / Week |
| --- | --- | --- | --- | --- |
| Mon | Rest / Cross-Train | Rest / Cross-Train | Easy Run | Easy Run |
| Tue | Threshold Session | Threshold Session | Threshold Session | Threshold Session |
| Wed | Rest | Easy Run | Easy Run | Easy Run |
| Thu | Easy Run | Rest | Easy Run or Strides | Easy Run or Strides |
| Fri | Rest | Easy Run | Rest or Easy Run | Rest |
| Sat | Rest | Rest | Easy Run | Easy Run |
| Sun | Long Run (Easy) | Long Run (Easy) | Long Run (Easy) | Long Run (Easy) |

Regardless of training frequency, quality sessions should always be separated by at least one easy day, and easy days should remain truly easy. When fatigue accumulates, reducing intensity is usually more effective than reducing overall consistency.

## How Half Marathon Training Differs From 10K Training

While both distances rely heavily on aerobic fitness, half marathon training places greater emphasis on sustained steady efforts and long-run endurance. Threshold sessions remain important, but a larger portion of training stress comes from longer aerobic work rather than short, intense intervals.

High-intensity sessions play a smaller role compared to 10K training. Speed is rarely the limiting factor in half marathon performance. Instead, success depends on maintaining efficient form and controlled pacing as fatigue builds.

Because of this, many half marathon improvements come not from running faster in workouts, but from running longer at controlled aerobic intensity and recovering well enough to repeat those efforts week after week.

Ultimately, half marathon preparation rewards patience and consistency. Runners who respect easy days, progress gradually, and maintain steady aerobic training often see stronger and more reliable improvements than those who rely on sporadic hard workouts.

In the next chapter, we'll look at how to adjust long runs to improve endurance without sacrificing speed, and how to integrate quality work into long runs safely and effectively.

# TWENTY-FIVE

# How to Adjust Long Runs Without Losing Speed

Long runs are often viewed as slow, purely endurance-focused sessions, but within Norwegian-style training they serve a more flexible and strategic role. While most long runs should remain easy, carefully placed moderate and steady efforts can improve fatigue resistance and race-specific strength without turning the run into a second hard workout.

The primary purpose of the long run is still aerobic development. Running for extended periods at comfortable intensity increases capillary density, strengthens connective tissues, improves fat utilization, and builds the durability needed to tolerate higher training volumes. These adaptations occur best when the pace remains relaxed enough that recovery is not compromised in the following days.

However, for runners preparing for longer races such as the 10K and half marathon, staying entirely easy on every long run may leave some endurance adaptations underdeveloped. This is where controlled pace variations can be added to long runs without changing their overall character.

One common approach is to include short steady segments within an otherwise easy long run. These segments are run slightly faster than easy pace but still below threshold intensity. For most runners, steady pace is roughly 20 to 40 seconds per kilometer slower than threshold pace, or a pace that feels clearly stronger than easy running but still fully controlled. Breathing becomes deeper and more noticeable, and conversation is limited to short phrases rather than full sentences (example: "Feeling strong… but I would not want to hold this pace all day"). The effort should feel purposeful but not strained, and runners should feel confident they could continue for quite a while if needed. The goal is to gently challenge aerobic endurance under light fatigue without creating the stress or recovery demands associated with threshold training.

For example, a runner might complete a 90-minute long run where the first 70 minutes are run easy, followed by the final 20 minutes at steady aerobic pace. Another option is to insert two or three steady blocks of 10 minutes, each separated by 10 to 15 minutes of easy running. During these steady segments, breathing should be strong but controlled, and pacing should feel smooth rather than forced. These formats improve the ability to hold form and rhythm as fatigue builds, which is especially important in the later stages of races, without turning the long run into a hard workout that requires extra recovery.

A second option is to progress the pace gradually across the entire long run. Instead of running every mile at the same easy speed, the first half remains very relaxed, while the second half becomes moderately faster but still controlled. This teaches the body to respond to increasing effort without requiring a dramatic pace change.

What should be avoided is turning the long run into a full threshold session or repeated hard intervals. Once intensity rises too high, the run stops functioning as a recovery-supportive endurance session and begins to compete with threshold workouts for recovery resources. This often leads to cumulative fatigue and reduced quality in the following week's training.

The placement of moderate segments also matters. Early in training blocks, most long runs should remain entirely easy to build volume safely. As race preparation progresses, steady segments can appear more frequently, but usually no more than once per week. Long runs that include pace work should still be followed by easier training days to allow recovery.

For long runs that extend beyond seventy to ninety minutes, carrying simple carbohydrates becomes useful for keeping effort steady and protecting recovery. While gels and chews are common, many runners also use everyday options such as dates, raisins, or dried apricots, which are easy to carry in a pocket and simple to eat while moving. The goal is not to eat a full meal, but to provide a small, steady supply of carbohydrates so that moderate-effort segments of the run can be completed without drifting into heavy fatigue.

Just as important as fueling is consistency. Race day is not the time to experiment with new foods, new gels, different brands or flavors, or unfamiliar drinks. The digestive system can react unpredictably under race stress and higher intensity, even to products that seem harmless in everyday life. For this reason, any fueling strategy used in races should first be tested during training, especially on long runs and steady sessions that simulate race effort. If something causes stomach discomfort in training, it's very unlikely to improve on race day.

The goal is for race day to feel like a slightly sharper version of a normal training day, not a completely different experience. Practicing fueling, pacing, and effort in training removes uncertainty and allows performance to reflect fitness rather than trial-and-error decisions.

For runners training multiple days per week, long runs should be viewed as part of the overall weekly stress balance. If the week already includes two demanding threshold sessions, the long run should remain mostly easy. If only one quality session is present, a slightly more demanding long run can provide additional aerobic stimulus without exceeding recovery capacity.

Ultimately, the goal of long-run progression is not to run harder, but to tolerate longer durations and mild fatigue while maintaining relaxed mechanics. This supports threshold training rather than replacing it, allowing aerobic fitness to improve across multiple systems simultaneously.

By keeping most long runs easy and using steady segments sparingly and strategically, runners can improve endurance without sacrificing speed, recovery, or consistency. This balance is what allows Norwegian-style training to scale across different race distances without dramatically changing weekly structure.

In the next chapter, we'll first cover how to taper before races so fatigue drops without losing fitness, then explain how training blocks are used to build progress over time instead of chasing short-term gains.

# TWENTY-SIX

# Tapering and Training Blocks

Tapering is the process of reducing training volume before a race so that fatigue drops while fitness is preserved. When done correctly, tapering allows runners to arrive at the start line feeling fresh, sharp, and confident without losing the aerobic strength built over months of training. When done poorly, it can leave runners feeling flat, sluggish, or anxious that they are "losing fitness."

One of the most common mistakes runners make during taper is cutting intensity instead of volume. Fitness is maintained by keeping some quality in the training week, while fatigue is reduced by lowering total mileage and shortening workouts. Eliminating threshold work entirely or replacing all quality sessions with very easy running often leads to a feeling of heaviness and dull legs on race day.

In the Norwegian approach, tapering focuses on keeping threshold and steady aerobic sessions in place, but reducing how much total work is done. Intervals may be shortened, the number of repeats reduced, and long runs trimmed, but effort levels remain familiar and controlled. This preserves the body's sense of rhythm and pacing while allowing accumulated fatigue to fade.

For most runners, overall weekly volume is reduced by about 15-30% in the final one to two weeks before a goal race. Easy runs become slightly shorter, and long runs are reduced in duration, but they are not eliminated entirely. This helps maintain routine and keeps the body moving without creating additional stress.

Threshold sessions during taper should feel comfortable and controlled. Instead of accumulating thirty or forty minutes of threshold work, runners may perform fifteen to twenty-five minutes in total, using the same pacing and structure as in regular training. This maintains aerobic sharpness without adding fatigue.

High-intensity sessions, if they are part of the program, should be used cautiously during taper. Short strides or very brief fast intervals may be included to maintain coordination and leg turnover, but long or exhausting interval workouts are usually unnecessary and counterproductive at this stage.

Another important part of tapering is resisting the urge to "test fitness" with hard workouts close to race day. Fitness gains occur during the weeks of training leading into taper, not during the final few days. Trying to prove readiness with aggressive sessions often increases fatigue without improving performance.

Sleep, nutrition, and stress management also become more important during taper. As physical training load drops, the body uses this time to complete recovery processes that were postponed during heavy training. Poor sleep, under-fueling, or excessive daily stress can blunt the benefits of taper and leave runners feeling less prepared than expected.

Mentally, taper can feel uncomfortable because reduced training volume may create anxiety or restlessness. Many runners worry that they are not doing enough. In reality, this rest is exactly what allows fitness to express itself on race day. Trusting the process is part of successful tapering.

The goal of taper is not to feel hyper-energized or restless, but to feel steady, relaxed, and ready. Legs may feel lighter, breathing easier, and pacing more controlled. These are signs that the body is shedding fatigue and preparing to perform.

When taper is approached as a gradual shift rather than a sudden stop, runners are far more likely to arrive at the start line confident and physically prepared. Fitness does not disappear in a week or two. What disappears is the fatigue that was masking it.

## What Is a Training Block and Why Length Matters

A training block is simply a planned stretch of weeks where your weekly structure stays mostly the same while key workouts progress gradually. Instead of changing workouts every few days, the body is given time to adapt to similar types of stress, which is what actually leads to improvement.

In a typical block, the main sessions stay consistent in purpose. Threshold workouts remain threshold focused, long runs remain long runs, and easy days stay easy. What changes from week to week is not the type of training, but the amount. Threshold sessions slowly increase in total work time, long runs gradually extend, and steady segments may be added later in the block once the body is handling the base workload well.

This gradual progression is what allows fitness to build without overwhelming recovery. Jumping too quickly in volume or intensity often leads to soreness, heavy legs, or stalled performance, even if motivation is high. Small weekly increases give the body a clear signal to adapt while keeping fatigue under control.

In most endurance programs, blocks typically last between six and twelve weeks depending on the goal. Shorter blocks around eight weeks are often used when the focus is on speed and aerobic power, such as during 5K preparation. Slightly longer blocks around ten weeks work well for 10K training, where sustained aerobic strength becomes more important. For the half marathon, where fatigue resistance and long-run durability are major performance factors, blocks of twelve weeks allow progress to happen more safely and steadily.

Blocks are not meant to be rigid. If workouts are still improving, recovery feels strong, and pacing is becoming more stable, a runner may repeat the final weeks of a block rather than increasing again immediately. This allows the body to fully absorb the training stress instead of forcing constant escalation. Many adaptations, especially in connective tissue and aerobic efficiency, continue to improve even when the workload stays the same.

Repeating also reduces injury risk and supports long-term consistency. Increasing long runs or threshold volume too aggressively is one of the most common reasons runners break down. Holding the same structure for a few extra weeks often produces better long-term progress than rushing into the next level of difficulty.

Motivation also plays a role. Training that constantly demands more can become mentally draining, even if the body is coping. Repeating a stable block can restore confidence, reduce stress, and help runners stay engaged rather than feeling like every week must be harder than the last.

When training is organized into blocks like this, improvement becomes more predictable. Instead of hoping that random hard workouts produce results, runners follow a steady progression that compounds over time. Fitness builds in layers, with each block supporting the next, rather than constantly resetting from fatigue, frustration, or minor setbacks.

In the next section, we'll put this structure into practice with complete training plans, showing exactly how weekly schedules and workout progressions change for different race distances and training frequencies.

PART VI
Putting It All Together

# TWENTY-SEVEN

# The Training Plans

The goal of these plans is to turn the Norwegian training principles into simple, repeatable weeks that fit real-world schedules. Instead of relying on extreme workouts, these plans emphasize controlled threshold training, consistent easy running, and gradual progression over time.

All sessions are prescribed using time and effort rather than distance, making them suitable for runners of different speeds. Use your most recent race results as a reference if needed, but always prioritize breathing, pacing stability, and recovery when deciding how hard to run.

Before starting any plan, runners should be able to run comfortably for at least thirty minutes and should be free from injury. If returning from time off, volumes should be reduced until consistency is re-established.

Across all versions of this plan, two sessions remain the anchors of the week: a threshold workout and a long aerobic run. These sessions drive most of the fitness gains. Easy runs exist to support recovery and build aerobic capacity, not to replace quality training.

**Warm-Ups and Cool-Downs: Small Habits That Protect Long-Term Progress**

Warm-ups and cool-downs are often treated as optional extras, but they play a major role in whether runners stay healthy and are able to train consistently. They reduce injury risk, improve the quality of harder sessions, and help the body recover faster so that training can be repeated week after week. No training plan works if it cannot be followed consistently, and consistency is almost always limited by injury and fatigue rather than motivation.

In an ideal situation, runners would spend about ten to fifteen minutes warming up and cooling down before and after harder workouts. This allows heart rate, breathing, and muscle temperature to rise and fall gradually, which reduces strain on muscles, tendons, and joints. It also gives the nervous system time to adapt to faster movement, improving coordination and running efficiency once the main workout begins.

That said, most recreational runners are balancing training with work, family, and limited time. Adding thirty extra minutes to every workout is often unrealistic. The good news is that even shorter warm-ups and cool-downs provide meaningful protection and are far better than skipping them altogether. Five to ten minutes of easy jogging before and after harder sessions can significantly reduce mechanical stress and improve recovery compared to starting and stopping abruptly.

A warm-up gradually increases blood flow and muscle temperature, making tissues more elastic and better able to handle faster running. It also allows breathing to settle and posture to improve before harder efforts begin. Jumping straight into threshold or faster running with cold muscles increases the risk of muscle strains and tendon irritation and often makes the first few minutes of a workout feel unnecessarily uncomfortable.

When time allows, starting with ten to fifteen minutes of easy jogging is ideal. When time is limited, five to eight minutes of easy jogging is usually enough to prepare the body safely. After this, adding two to four short strides lasting about fifteen to twenty seconds helps prepare the nervous system for faster movement. These strides should gradually build speed while remaining relaxed and controlled, followed by easy walking or jogging for about forty-five to sixty seconds between each effort. Strides should never feel like sprints, and they should not leave runners breathless or fatigued.

Cool-downs serve a different but equally important purpose. They help the body transition gradually from higher effort back to resting state, supporting circulation and helping clear metabolic byproducts from working muscles. While cool-downs don't directly increase fitness, they improve recovery quality, which affects how well runners can train again in the following days.

Without cool-downs, heart rate and muscle tension drop abruptly, which can contribute to stiffness and lingering soreness later in the day. Over time, this low-level fatigue can accumulate and interfere with training consistency. Even five to ten minutes of very easy jogging after harder sessions can help reduce stiffness and improve how the legs feel the next day.

After the easy jog, light stretching or gentle mobility can be added if it feels helpful, especially for calves, hamstrings, hips, and lower back. Stretching should feel relaxed and should never be forced or painful. The goal is simply to restore comfortable movement rather than to push flexibility.

Warm-ups and cool-downs are not about making workouts longer or harder. They are about protecting the ability to train tomorrow, next week, and next month.

When runners stay healthy, they can repeat quality training sessions consistently. When training is consistent, fitness improves naturally. Warm-ups and cool-downs quietly support this process in the background, even though they rarely receive much attention. Their main purpose is not to improve fitness directly, but to protect the body so that training can continue without interruption.

For easy runs and most long runs, the beginning of the run can serve as the warm-up. As long as the first five to ten minutes are kept very relaxed, the body has time to ease into movement, breathing settles, and muscles gradually become ready for sustained running. There is no need to stop and perform a separate warm-up routine before these types of sessions, as long as runners resist the urge to start too fast.

This is also why long runs should always begin gently, even when steady segments are planned later in the run. Starting too fast increases fatigue early and raises injury risk without providing extra fitness benefit. Allowing the body to warm up naturally before settling into rhythm makes the entire run smoother and easier to recover from.

Harder sessions are different. When a workout includes threshold running, steady aerobic efforts, hills, or faster intervals, the body needs more preparation before intensity begins. In these cases, relying on the first few minutes of faster running to act as the warm-up increases mechanical stress and makes the session feel harder than it needs to be. This is where a short, intentional warm-up before the main workout becomes important.

Cool-downs follow the same logic. Easy runs naturally taper down as pace remains relaxed throughout, but harder sessions benefit from a few minutes of very easy jogging afterward to help the body settle back to normal. This reduces stiffness and supports recovery so the next training day feels smoother rather than heavy or tight.

A simple guideline is helpful to remember. If a session includes controlled or faster running, it should always include a warm-up and a cool-down. If a session is easy or a long aerobic run, it should start easy and finish easy. This small habit dramatically improves the chances that training remains sustainable over the long term without adding unnecessary time or complexity.

# TWENTY-EIGHT

# 8-Week 5K Training Plan

This plan is designed to improve aerobic strength, pacing control, and finishing ability for the 5K while keeping fatigue manageable and recovery reliable. Threshold training forms the backbone of the program, supported by easy running, long runs, and small amounts of sharpening work as race day approaches.

Use your most recent 5K result from the past six to eight weeks to guide pacing when needed, but effort and breathing cues should always take priority over exact numbers.

Because the 5K is short and easy to measure, it is also one of the simplest distances to use for testing progress. Runners who do not have an upcoming race can perform their own 5K time trial before starting the plan and repeat it after completing the eight weeks. To make the comparison meaningful, it is important to keep conditions as similar as possible between tests. Ideally, choose a flat route or track where pacing is not affected by hills or sharp turns, and aim for calm weather without strong wind, heavy rain, or extreme heat. Cooler temperatures generally support better performance, as the body does not need to divert as much energy toward cooling.

Time of day also matters more than many runners realize. Testing at a similar time, such as early morning or early evening, helps reduce the effects of daily fatigue, hydration differences, and body temperature fluctuations. Wearing similar shoes and running on the same surface further improves consistency. The goal is not to create perfect laboratory conditions, but to reduce unnecessary variables so that changes in performance reflect fitness rather than environment.

By repeating the test under similar conditions, runners can get a clearer picture of how much they have improved from the training block. Even small time reductions over 5 kilometers represent meaningful fitness gains and often translate into improved endurance, smoother pacing, and better recovery in regular training. This type of simple, repeatable testing reinforces the idea that progress comes from consistent work over time, not from any single workout.

**How much faster could I realistically get?**

Runners often ask how much improvement they should expect from a training block like this. While individual responses vary, many recreational runners see noticeable gains within one cycle, often improving their 5K time by thirty seconds to two minutes after eight weeks of consistent training. The amount of improvement is strongly influenced by starting fitness and training background.

Runners currently finishing in the thirty-minute range or slower often see larger short-term gains, sometimes improving by two to four minutes in a single training block, especially if they previously trained inconsistently or without structured threshold work. Runners in the low- to mid-twenties more commonly see improvements of about one to two minutes. For runners already in the teens, gains are usually smaller in absolute time, often around thirty to ninety seconds, but these improvements represent significant performance jumps at higher levels of fitness.

Training frequency also plays a role in how much improvement runners may see within a single block, though the difference is usually modest rather than dramatic. Many runners training three days per week improve by about thirty seconds to two minutes over 5K in one eight-week cycle. Adding a fourth day often leads to slightly larger gains, commonly an additional ten to thirty seconds within the same block, assuming recovery remains strong. Moving to five days per week may add another small improvement, again often in the range of ten to thirty seconds, for runners who tolerate the extra volume without sacrificing pacing quality or recovery.

Progress also depends on several other factors, including training history, recovery habits, sleep, nutrition, stress levels, and how consistently the plan is followed. Runners who are newer to structured training often improve more quickly, while experienced runners may see smaller but still meaningful gains that become harder to achieve and more valuable as fitness increases.

It is also important to recognize that improvement does not always appear first as a dramatic race result. Many runners initially notice progress through smoother pacing, lower perceived effort at familiar speeds, and better recovery between sessions. These changes often signal that fitness is improving even before race times fully reflect it.

The goal of this plan is not short-term breakthroughs, but building a foundation that can support repeated training cycles and long-term development. When this type of training is repeated across multiple blocks, improvements tend to compound over time, leading to far greater gains across a full year than any single cycle can produce.

## Primary Option – 3 Days Per Week

| Day | Session | Notes |
| --- | --- | --- |
| Tuesday | Threshold | Follow the threshold progression plan |
| Thursday | Easy Run | 30–45 min, relaxed conversational pace |
| Saturday | Long Run | Follow the long-run progression plan |
| Other days | Rest or Easy Cross-Training (optional) | Cycling, swimming, rowing, elliptical at easy effort |

This structure is ideal for runners with limited training time or those returning to consistent running. The focus is on one quality session, one long run, and one easy run each week. Easy cross-training may be added on other days if desired.


**Threshold Session Progression**

In the workouts below, the time in brackets refers to the easy jogging recovery taken between each threshold repeat.

Week 1 — 4 × 5 min (90 sec easy jog)

Run 5 minutes at threshold, then jog easily for 90 seconds. Repeat 4 times.

Week 2 — 2 × 10 min (2 min easy jog)

Week 3 — 3 × 8 min (90 sec easy jog)

Week 4 — 1 × 25 min steady threshold

Week 5 — 4 × 8 min (60–90 sec easy jog)

Week 6 — 2 × 15 min (2 min easy jog)

Week 7 — 3 × 5 min (taper)

Week 8 — 1 × 15–20 min very controlled (race week)

All threshold sessions should feel "comfortably hard." Breathing is deep and focused, but not panicked, and the pace feels strong yet sustainable. Runners should feel in control of the effort rather than fighting to hold the speed. If speaking is possible only in short phrases, pacing is likely correct. If full sentences come easily, the effort is probably too easy. If even short phrases are difficult or pacing drops sharply, the effort is likely too hard and should be backed off slightly.


**Long Run Progression**

Week 1 — 50 min

Week 2 — 55 min

Week 3 — 60 min

Week 4 — 65 min

Week 5 — 70 min

Week 6 — 75 min

Week 7 — 50 min

Week 8 — 30–40 min early in race week only

**Easy Runs**

Thursday runs should be 30–45 minutes at a relaxed conversational pace.

## Secondary Option – 4 Days Per Week

This structure is ideal for runners who can train more frequently and want to increase aerobic volume without adding more intensity. The goal is not to work harder, but to recover better and build endurance more consistently across the week.

Threshold sessions and long runs remain exactly the same as in the 3-day plan. The only difference is the addition of one extra easy run, which supports recovery and gradually increases overall aerobic fitness.

Weekly Structure

| Day | Session | Notes |
| --- | --- | --- |
| Monday | Easy Run | 30–50 min, relaxed conversational pace |
| Wednesday | Threshold | Same threshold progression as 3-day plan |
| Friday | Easy Run | Easy and relaxed, not a workout |
| Sunday | Long Run | Same long-run progression as 3-day plan |

This layout spaces demanding sessions apart and keeps easy days truly easy. Days can be shifted to match personal schedules, but threshold and long runs should always be separated by at least one easy day.

The added easy run should be performed at relaxed conversational pace and typically last 30–50 minutes. It should never feel like a workout. If this run begins to feel tiring or starts affecting the quality of threshold sessions, overall weekly stress is likely too high.

**Why the Extra Day Helps**

Adding a fourth day of running increases total aerobic volume and improves how well the body absorbs harder sessions. Over multiple training blocks, runners who tolerate four days per week often build fitness more steadily and experience fewer setbacks from fatigue or minor injuries.

In terms of race results, short-term improvements over a single 8-week block may be similar to the 3-day plan, especially for newer runners. However, runners in the low- to mid-twenties and faster often benefit more from added consistency than from adding extra intensity. Over several training cycles, this additional volume can lead to more reliable long-term progress.

As a rough guide, runners who complete the plan on four days per week instead of three often see an additional 10 to 30 seconds of improvement compared to lower-frequency training, assuming recovery remains strong and training is consistent. While this may seem small, it becomes increasingly meaningful as fitness improves and larger gains are harder to achieve.

Runners should only move to four days per week if recovery remains solid. If threshold sessions become harder to control or easy runs stop feeling easy, returning temporarily to three days per week is often the smarter choice.

## 5 Days Per Week – Weekly Structure

| Day | Session | Notes |
| --- | --- | --- |
| Monday | Easy Run | 30–50 min, relaxed conversational pace |
| Tuesday | Threshold | Follow the threshold progression plan |
| Thursday | Easy Run | Easy and relaxed, supports recovery |
| Saturday | Steady / Light Quality or Easy Run | Steady aerobic (optional) or easy if fatigued |
| Sunday | Long Run | Follow the long-run progression plan |

**What Changes From 4 Days Per Week**

Threshold sessions and long runs remain the primary quality drivers. The fifth day adds either:

• more easy aerobic volume, or

• a light steady aerobic stimulus slightly below threshold

This extra day improves aerobic durability and allows runners to tolerate more total training without increasing high-intensity stress.

**About the Steady Run Option (Saturday)**

When used, the steady run should feel comfortably controlled and clearly easier than threshold. Breathing should be deeper than easy running but still fully manageable, and pace should feel sustainable for a long time.

**Typical duration:**

30–50 minutes depending on fitness and weekly fatigue.

If legs feel heavy, recovery is poor, or threshold sessions start to suffer, this run should remain fully easy instead of steady.

**Why 5 Days Can Help Performance**

Running five days per week improves aerobic development primarily by increasing frequency and total volume, not by adding harder workouts. Over time, this leads to better fatigue resistance and more consistent pacing late in races.

Short-term improvements over a single 8-week block may be similar to four days per week, but runners who tolerate five days often see stronger long-term progress across multiple training cycles.

As a rough guide, runners who successfully move from four to five days per week and maintain good recovery may see an additional 10–30 seconds of improvement over 5K across a full season of training, rather than within a single block. At higher fitness levels, this type of gain becomes increasingly meaningful.

**When Not to Use 5 Days Per Week**

Runners should not increase frequency if:

• easy runs no longer feel easy

• threshold pacing becomes harder to control

• soreness or minor injuries start to appear

In these cases, returning temporarily to four days per week usually leads to better overall progress than forcing extra mileage.

# TWENTY-NINE

# 10-Week 10K Training Plan

This plan is designed to improve sustained aerobic strength, pacing stability, and late-race durability for the 10K while keeping fatigue manageable and recovery reliable. As with the 5K plan, threshold training remains the backbone of the program, supported by easy running, long runs, and small amounts of sharpening work as race day approaches.

Use your most recent 10K result from the past six to eight weeks to guide pacing when needed, but effort and breathing cues should always take priority over exact numbers.

Because the 10K is still short enough to test without excessive recovery, runners who do not have an upcoming race can perform a controlled 10K time trial before starting the plan and repeat it after completing the ten weeks. To make comparisons meaningful, testing conditions should be kept as similar as possible. A flat route or track, calm weather, moderate temperatures, and a similar time of day all help ensure that improvements reflect fitness rather than external factors.

Even small time reductions over 10 kilometers represent meaningful gains in aerobic strength and endurance. Improvements also tend to show up as steadier pacing, less late-race fatigue, and better recovery between quality sessions.

## How Much Faster Could I Realistically Get?

Many recreational runners improve their 10K performance by about forty-five seconds to three minutes over a single ten-week training block when training consistently and recovering well. The amount of improvement depends strongly on starting fitness, recent training history, and how well threshold and long runs are absorbed.

Runners finishing in the fifty- to sixty-minute range often see larger short-term gains, sometimes improving by two to four minutes in one block, especially if previous training lacked structured threshold work or consistent long runs. Runners around the forty-minute mark more commonly improve by about one to two minutes. For runners already in the mid- to high-thirty-minute range, improvements are usually smaller in absolute time, often around thirty to ninety seconds, but these gains represent meaningful performance increases at higher fitness levels.

Training frequency can also influence results within a single block, though the differences are usually modest. Many runners training three days per week improve their 10K time by about forty-five seconds to two minutes over a ten-week cycle. Adding a fourth day may lead to slightly larger gains, often an additional fifteen to forty-five seconds, assuming recovery remains strong and easy days stay truly easy. Moving to five days per week may add another small improvement in a similar range for runners who tolerate the extra volume without sacrificing pacing quality or recovery.

The biggest advantage of higher frequency is not dramatic short-term improvement within one block, but the ability to build fitness more steadily across multiple training cycles. Over time, this consistency often leads to greater long-term gains than simply trying to make one block as hard as possible.

Progress also depends on sleep, nutrition, stress, and how consistently training is completed. As fitness improves, gains tend to become more gradual, but repeated well-managed training blocks usually lead to steady long-term development across a season rather than dramatic changes in any single cycle.

It is also worth noting that improvements may first appear as smoother pacing, lower effort at familiar speeds, and stronger finishes in long runs before they show up clearly in race results. These signs often indicate that aerobic fitness is improving even when race times have not yet shifted dramatically.

## Primary Option – 3 Days Per Week

This structure is ideal for runners with limited training time who still want to build strong 10K fitness. Each week includes one threshold workout, one easy run, and one long run.

### Weekly Structure

| Day | Session | Notes |
| --- | --- | --- |
| Tuesday | Threshold | Follow the threshold progression plan |
| Thursday | Easy Run | 30–45 min, relaxed conversational pace |
| Sunday | Long Run | Follow the long-run progression plan (easy pace throughout) |
| Other days | Rest or Easy Cross-Training (optional) | Cycling, swimming, rowing, elliptical at easy effort |

Easy cross-training may be added on other days if desired, as long as it does not interfere with recovery.

**Threshold Session Progression**

In the workouts below, the time in brackets refers to the easy jogging recovery taken between each threshold repeat.

Week 1 — 3 × 8 min (90 sec easy jog)

Run 8 minutes at threshold, then jog easily for 90 seconds. Repeat 3 times.

Week 2 — 2 × 12 min (2 min easy jog)

Week 3 — 3 × 10 min (90 sec easy jog)

Week 4 — 1 × 30 min steady threshold

Week 5 — 4 × 8 min (60–90 sec easy jog)

Week 6 — 2 × 15 min (2 min easy jog)

Week 7 — 3 × 10 min (90 sec easy jog)

Week 8 — 1 × 35 min steady threshold

Week 9 — 3 × 6 min (taper)

Week 10 — 1 × 15–20 min very controlled (race week)

All threshold sessions should feel comfortably hard and repeatable. Breathing should be strong but controlled, and pacing should remain stable across all repeats.


**Long Run Progression**

Week 1 — 65 min

Week 2 — 70 min

Week 3 — 75 min

Week 4 — 80 min

Week 5 — 85 min

Week 6 — 90 min

Week 7 — 85 min

Week 8 — 90 min with last 10 min steady (optional)

Week 9 — 65 min

Week 10 — 40–50 min early in race week only

Long runs should remain mostly easy. Optional steady segments should only be added if recovery has been strong and legs feel fresh.

## Easy Runs

Easy runs should last 35–50 minutes at relaxed conversational pace.

## Secondary Option – 4 Days Per Week

This structure increases aerobic volume without adding intensity. Threshold sessions and long runs remain exactly the same as in the 3-day plan. The only change is the addition of one extra easy run.

### Weekly Structure

| Day | Session | Notes |
| --- | --- | --- |
| Tuesday | Threshold | Follow the threshold progression plan |
| Wednesday | Easy Run | 30–45 min, relaxed conversational pace |
| Friday | Easy Run | 30–45 min, relaxed conversational pace |
| Sunday | Long Run | Follow the long-run progression plan (easy pace throughout) |
| Other days | Rest or Easy Cross-Training (optional) | Low-impact aerobic work at easy effort |

The added easy run should remain fully relaxed and last about 30–50 minutes. If this run begins to affect recovery or threshold pacing, overall weekly stress is likely too high.

Over multiple training cycles, runners who tolerate four days per week often build fitness more steadily than those training fewer days. Short-term gains over a single block may be similar to three days per week, but long-term development tends to improve with increased consistency.

As a rough guide, runners who move from three to four days per week and maintain good recovery often see an additional thirty seconds to one minute of improvement over 10K across a full season of training rather than within a single ten-week block. For runners already in the forty-minute range or faster, even thirty seconds can represent a meaningful performance gain.

The main benefit of the extra day is not that workouts become harder, but that aerobic volume increases without raising intensity. This improves fatigue resistance, helps stabilize pacing late in races, and reduces the chance that fitness drops between training blocks.

Runners should only move to four days per week if easy runs remain easy and threshold pacing stays controlled. If fatigue begins to accumulate or recovery declines, returning temporarily to three days per week often leads to better overall progress than forcing extra mileage.

## Tertiary Option – 5 Days Per Week

This option is best suited for runners who already tolerate regular training and recover well between sessions. Threshold and long runs remain the anchors of the week, while added easy running builds aerobic durability.

**Weekly Structure**

| Day | Session | Notes |
| --- | --- | --- |
| Monday | Easy Run | 30–45 min, relaxed conversational pace |
| Tuesday | Threshold | Follow the threshold progression plan |
| Wednesday | Easy Run | 30–45 min, relaxed conversational pace |
| Thursday | Rest | Full rest day |
| Friday | Rest or Easy Run | Rest if tired; otherwise 25–40 min easy |
| Saturday | Easy Run | 30–45 min, relaxed conversational pace |
| Sunday | Long Run | Follow the long-run progression plan at easy pace |

A steady run sits between easy pace and threshold. It feels purposeful and controlled, but not hard. Breathing is deeper than on easy runs, and conversation becomes limited to short sentences, but you are never straining to hold pace. You should feel like you are working, but comfortably, and could maintain the effort for quite a while. Steady runs build fatigue resistance and help bridge the gap between easy running and threshold training, especially for longer races like the 10K and half marathon.

If legs feel heavy or threshold sessions become harder to control, this day should remain fully easy instead of steady.

Over time, runners who tolerate five days per week often improve fatigue resistance and pacing consistency, especially in the later stages of races. Improvements tend to accumulate across multiple blocks rather than appearing immediately within a single cycle.


## Tapering and Race Preparation

In the final two weeks, overall training volume is reduced so that fatigue can drop while fitness is maintained. Threshold sessions become shorter, long runs are reduced, and easy runs remain relaxed. Intensity stays familiar, but total workload decreases to allow full recovery before race day.

The goal of taper is not to build new fitness, but to arrive at the start line feeling rested, confident, and sharp.

# THIRTY

# Training for the Half Marathon
# Using Norwegian Principles

By the time runners reach the half marathon, aerobic endurance becomes the dominant performance factor. The race is long enough that success depends far more on how well pace can be sustained than on how fast the legs can move for short periods. For this reason, half marathon training shifts toward longer controlled efforts with greater emphasis on fatigue resistance.

Threshold training remains important, but sessions typically become longer and more continuous than in 5K or 10K preparation. Rather than short repeats, half marathon threshold workouts often focus on building the ability to stay near threshold for extended periods without large fluctuations in pace or effort. This improves both physiological efficiency and pacing control, which are critical late in the race.

Typical threshold sessions for half marathon preparation accumulate roughly thirty to fifty minutes of total work at threshold intensity. This may be done using longer repeats such as three sets of twelve to fifteen minutes with short recoveries of about one to two minutes, or through continuous steady efforts lasting twenty-five to forty minutes. The goal is not to push harder, but to stay controlled for longer.

Steady aerobic running just below threshold also becomes more valuable at this distance. These efforts sit between easy pace and threshold and can be maintained for longer durations. Steady runs help develop the ability to hold form and rhythm when tired, which directly carries over to the later stages of a half marathon when fatigue begins to affect pacing.

Long runs become a more central part of performance preparation. Beyond building general endurance, they improve muscular resilience, connective tissue strength, and the body's ability to use fuel efficiently over time. Most runners benefit from long runs lasting about ninety to one hundred forty minutes, with occasional steady segments added during later training phases to improve fatigue tolerance without turning the run into a full race simulation.

High-intensity sessions play a much smaller role compared to shorter race distances. While short intervals or hill work can still be included occasionally to maintain coordination and leg strength, they are not a primary driver of half marathon performance and should never compromise threshold or long-run quality.

For pacing reference, recent 10K race results are usually the most useful guide for setting training speeds during half marathon preparation, as they reflect sustained aerobic ability more accurately than shorter races. When recent race data is not available, effort and breathing cues should always guide intensity rather than rigid pace targets.

**Half Marathon Training Pace Guide (Based on Recent 10K Time)**

| 10K Time | 10K Pace | Threshold Pace | Steady Aerobic Pace | Easy Run Pace |
| --- | --- | --- | --- | --- |
| 30:00 | 4:49/mi (3:00/km) | 5:05–5:20/mi (3:10–3:20/km) | 5:30–5:50/mi (3:25–3:38/km) | 6:10–7:00/mi (3:50–4:20/km) |
| 35:00 | 5:38/mi (3:30/km) | 6:00–6:15/mi (3:44–3:54/km) | 6:30–6:50/mi (4:02–4:15/km) | 7:00–8:00/mi (4:20–5:00/km) |
| 40:00 | 6:26/mi (4:00/km) | 6:50–7:05/mi (4:15–4:25/km) | 7:15–7:40/mi (4:30–4:45/km) | 8:00–9:00/mi (5:00–5:35/km) |
| 45:00 | 7:14/mi (4:30/km) | 7:40–8:00/mi (4:45–5:00/km) | 8:10–8:40/mi (5:05–5:25/km) | 9:00–10:00/mi (5:35–6:10/km) |
| 50:00 | 8:03/mi (5:00/km) | 8:30–8:55/mi (5:15–5:30/km) | 9:00–9:40/mi (5:35–6:00/km) | 10:00–11:00/mi (6:10–6:50/km) |
| 55:00 | 8:51/mi (5:30/km) | 9:20–9:45/mi (5:50–6:05/km) | 10:00–10:40/mi (6:10–6:40/km) | 11:00–12:00/mi (6:50–7:30/km) |
| 60:00 | 9:39/mi (6:00/km) | 10:10–10:35/mi (6:20–6:35/km) | 10:50–11:30/mi (6:45–7:10/km) | 12:00–13:00/mi (7:30–8:05/km) |
| 70:00 | 11:16/mi (7:00/km) | 11:45–12:15/mi (7:18–7:38/km) | 12:30–13:20/mi (7:45–8:15/km) | 13:30–15:00/mi (8:25–9:20/km) |
| 80:00 | 12:52/mi (8:00/km) | 13:30–14:15/mi (8:24–8:50/km) | 14:20–15:30/mi (8:55–9:40/km) | 15:30–17:00/mi (9:40–10:35/km) |

As race day approaches, training becomes more specific without changing its overall structure. Threshold efforts may move slightly closer to expected race pace, steady segments may appear more often within long runs, and total weekly volume is usually reduced modestly to allow fatigue to drop. The aim is to arrive at the start line with fitness fully intact and legs that feel rested rather than overworked.

## Why This Plan Uses a 10-Week Structure

Half marathon preparation requires enough time to safely build both threshold endurance and long-run durability without rushing progression. Shorter plans often force rapid increases in workload, which can compromise recovery and increase injury risk, especially when long runs and sustained threshold sessions are both increasing. A ten-week structure allows training stress to rise gradually, giving the body time to adapt to longer controlled efforts and extended aerobic work while maintaining consistency.

At the same time, plans that stretch much longer than ten to twelve weeks often become difficult to follow consistently due to fatigue, scheduling conflicts, and declining motivation. For most recreational runners, a focused ten-week block provides the right balance between meaningful progression and practical sustainability. It is long enough to build significant fitness, yet short enough to maintain momentum and arrive at race day feeling prepared rather than worn down.

## Half Marathon – 3 Days Per Week Plan

Best for runners with limited time or those who need more recovery between sessions.

| Day | Session | Notes |
| --- | --- | --- |
| Tuesday | Threshold | Follow the threshold progression plan |
| Thursday | Easy Run | 30–45 min, relaxed conversational pace |
| Sunday | Long Run | Follow the long-run progression plan at easy pace |
| Other days | Rest or Easy Cross-Training (optional) | Cycling, swimming, rowing, elliptical at easy effort |

**Threshold Session Progression**

In the workouts below, the time in brackets refers to the easy jogging recovery taken between each threshold repeat.

Week 1 — 3 × 8 min (90 sec easy jog)

Run 8 minutes at threshold, then jog easily for 90 seconds. Repeat 3 times.

Week 2 — 3 × 9 min (90 sec easy jog)

Week 3 — 3 × 10 min (90 sec easy jog)

Week 4 — 2 × 15 min (2 min easy jog)

Week 5 — 1 × 30 min steady threshold

Week 6 — 3 × 10 min (60–90 sec easy jog)

Week 7 — 2 × 18 min (2 min easy jog)

Week 8 — 1 × 35 min steady threshold

Week 9 — 3 × 6 min (taper)

Week 10 — 1 × 20 min very controlled (race week)

These shorter sessions maintain rhythm and confidence while allowing fatigue to drop before race day.

All threshold sessions should feel comfortably hard and repeatable. Breathing should be strong but controlled, and pacing should remain stable across all repeats. The goal is not to push speed, but to stay smooth and consistent for longer durations.

**Long Run Progression**

Long runs should remain mostly easy. Optional steady segments should only be added if recovery has been strong and legs feel fresh.

Week 1 — 65 min

Week 2 — 70 min

Week 3 — 75 min

Week 4 — 80 min

Week 5 — 85 min

Week 6 — 90 min

Week 7 — 85 min

Week 8 — 90 min with last 10 min steady (optional)

Week 9 — 65 min

Week 10 — 40–50 min early in race week only

The purpose of the long run is to build endurance and fatigue resistance, not to simulate race pace. Most of the run should feel relaxed, with any steady segments added cautiously and only in later weeks of the plan.

## Half Marathon – 4 Days Per Week Plan

Ideal for runners who can handle more volume without adding intensity.

| Day | Session | Notes |
| --- | --- | --- |
| Monday | Rest or Easy Cross-Training (optional) | Low-impact aerobic work at easy effort |
| Tuesday | Threshold | Follow the threshold progression plan |
| Wednesday | Easy Run | 30–45 min, relaxed conversational pace |
| Thursday | Rest | Full rest day |
| Friday | Easy Run | 30–45 min, relaxed conversational pace |
| Saturday | Rest | Full rest day |
| Sunday | Long Run | Follow the long-run progression plan at easy pace |

Threshold sessions and long runs remain the primary drivers of fitness in the four-day plan, just as they are in the three-day structure. The added easy run increases overall aerobic volume and improves recovery between quality sessions, which often allows runners to handle long runs and threshold workouts more comfortably and consistently. While short-term improvements over a single training block may look similar to those seen with three days per week, many runners find they tolerate slightly longer peak long runs, typically in the range of 90 to 110 minutes, and maintain better pacing control as fatigue builds. Over time, this improved durability supports steadier progress across multiple training cycles without increasing workout intensity.

## Half Marathon – 5 Days Per Week Plan

For runners with strong recovery and consistent training background.

| Day | Session | Notes |
| --- | --- | --- |
| Monday | Easy Run | 30–45 min, relaxed conversational pace |
| Tuesday | Threshold | Follow the threshold progression plan |
| Wednesday | Easy Run | 30–45 min, relaxed conversational pace |
| Thursday | Rest | Full rest day |
| Friday | Easy Run | 25–40 min, relaxed conversational pace |
| Saturday | Easy Run or Strides | Easy run; optional strides 4–8 × 15–25 sec |
| Sunday | Long Run | Follow the long-run progression plan at easy pace |

In the five-day structure, the steady aerobic run should feel clearly easier than threshold but more purposeful than an easy jog, helping build fatigue resistance without adding high-intensity stress. If recovery begins to slip or threshold pacing becomes harder to control, this run should remain fully easy rather than steady. Most of the benefit from five days per week comes from increased training frequency and total aerobic volume rather than harder workouts. Over multiple training cycles, runners often develop stronger fatigue resistance, more stable pacing late in races, and greater tolerance for longer threshold sessions. Long runs may gradually extend toward the upper end of the recommended range, typically peaking around one hundred to one hundred fifteen minutes depending on fitness and recovery, but longer is not automatically better, and long runs should never compromise threshold quality or overall weekly consistency.

## HOW MUCH FASTER COULD I REALISTICALLY GET?

Many recreational runners improve their half marathon performance by one to five minutes over a single ten-week training block when training consistently and recovering well. The amount of improvement depends strongly on starting fitness, training history, and how well the body adapts to increased endurance work.

Runners finishing in the two-hour to two-and-a-half-hour range often see the largest short-term gains, especially if previous training lacked structure, consistent long runs, or controlled threshold work. Improvements of eight to fifteen minutes over a single ten-week block are common in this group, and in some cases gains may be even larger when consistency and recovery improve at the same time.

Runners finishing around one hour forty to one hour fifty commonly improve by three to six minutes, depending on training history and how well long runs and threshold sessions are absorbed. At this level, aerobic fitness is already more developed, so progress tends to be steadier rather than dramatic.

For runners already near the ninety-minute mark, improvements are usually smaller in absolute time, often one to three minutes, but these gains represent significant performance increases when fitness is already high and pacing efficiency becomes the main limiter.

Training frequency can also influence results within a single training block, though the differences are usually modest rather than dramatic. Many runners training three days per week see strong improvements when threshold sessions and long runs are performed consistently. Adding a fourth day often produces slightly larger gains, commonly in the range of thirty seconds to one minute over the half marathon within the same block, assuming recovery remains strong. Moving to five days per week may add another small improvement for runners who tolerate the extra volume, but the advantage is usually subtle and depends heavily on maintaining easy days at truly easy intensity.

The biggest benefit of higher training frequency is not immediate time drops in a single race, but improved consistency across training weeks. Runners who can train more often without accumulating fatigue are better able to repeat quality sessions, progress long runs gradually, and avoid setbacks from soreness or minor injuries. Over multiple training cycles, this steady accumulation of aerobic work becomes far more important than squeezing out extra intensity.

For this reason, training frequency should be chosen based on lifestyle, recovery capacity, and consistency rather than on the assumption that more days automatically produce better results. Three days per week can already produce large gains when training is well structured. Four or five days per week may provide small additional benefits if recovery remains strong, but only when the extra volume does not interfere with the quality of key sessions.

Once the training plans begin, the focus shifts away from expected time improvements and toward what matters most on a weekly basis: what to run, how often to run, and how to progress safely from week to week. When training is repeated consistently, race performance tends to improve naturally without needing to chase specific time targets inside each plan.

# THIRTY-ONE

# How to Repeat and Progress Each Plan

Finishing a training plan does not mean fitness disappears or that training must restart from zero. Most long-term improvement comes from repeating similar training structures across multiple blocks while gradually increasing how much quality work the body can tolerate.

After a race or time trial, most runners benefit from several days to one week of reduced volume with only easy running. This allows fatigue to drop while keeping aerobic fitness intact. Once easy runs feel comfortable again and legs feel normal, structured training can resume.

Repeating the same plan is often the simplest and most effective option. Because the body already recognizes the structure, runners usually handle the workload more comfortably in the second cycle, hold steadier pacing in threshold sessions, and recover faster between workouts. This alone is enough to drive further improvement without changing the overall design of the program.

Progress should focus first on execution rather than adding more work. Signs of improvement include smoother pacing at the same efforts, better control late in long runs, and quicker recovery between sessions. These changes often appear before major race-time improvements and indicate that aerobic efficiency is increasing.

If recovery remains strong, small increases can be added in the next block. This may include slightly longer threshold intervals, an extra repeat in a session, or adding short steady segments to long runs more consistently. Only one variable should increase at a time so sessions remain repeatable and fatigue stays manageable.

Changing race distance doesn't require a complete reset. When moving from shorter to longer races, the main adjustment is gradually extending threshold work and long runs. When moving from longer to shorter races, threshold remains central but sessions may become slightly shorter, with occasional speed-focused work added to improve leg turnover. In both cases, overall weekly structure can stay largely the same.

Some runners benefit from a short reset phase of one to two weeks with only easy running if motivation is low or minor aches are building. This drop in stress often improves the quality of the next training block more than pushing straight into another structured plan.

As fitness improves, gains naturally become smaller and slower. This does not mean training has stopped working. At higher fitness levels, progress comes from steady consistency across multiple blocks rather than aggressive increases in workload.

Over the course of a year, most runners can complete several blocks that build on each other. Each cycle raises the level at which the body can train comfortably, allowing fitness to accumulate gradually rather than being repeatedly rebuilt after fatigue or injury.

Progress is not created by perfect individual weeks, but by stacking many solid weeks together. This is the core of long-term development and the foundation of the Norwegian approach.

# PART VII

# Staying Fast and Healthy Long Term

# THIRTY-TWO

# Building Year-Round Fitness Without Burnout

Many runners fall into the trap of treating every month like race season. Training becomes a constant cycle of hard workouts, tapering, racing, and then rushing straight back into another buildup. While this approach can produce short-term results, it often leads to fatigue, stalled progress, and eventually injury or burnout. Sustainable improvement comes from understanding that fitness is built across months and years, not just between race dates.

The Norwegian approach is built around the idea of consistency and repeatability rather than constant peak performance. Instead of always chasing race-day sharpness, most training is focused on building aerobic capacity and durability so that quality work can be repeated week after week. This makes it possible to improve steadily without needing frequent full recoveries from extreme efforts.

A helpful way to think about training across the year is in terms of training blocks rather than isolated races. Each block focuses on developing a specific set of qualities, followed by a short consolidation phase before moving into the next block. Some blocks may emphasize general aerobic development, others may focus more on threshold endurance, and later blocks may sharpen race-specific fitness. Not every block needs to end with a race. Many can simply aim to raise the overall baseline before the next phase begins.

Rotating goals across the year also helps reduce both physical and mental fatigue. Instead of training for the same race distance all year, runners may spend one part of the year focusing on shorter races, another on longer distances, and another on general fitness without a specific competition goal. This variation keeps training stimulating while spreading mechanical stress across different intensity ranges and pacing demands.

Constant race-mode training often creates a pattern of building fitness only to lose it again through repeated tapers and recovery periods. When races are stacked too closely together, training quality between them suffers, and fitness never fully stabilizes at a higher level. Fewer, more purposeful race periods with longer development phases in between typically produce better long-term results than chasing frequent competition.

Another key part of avoiding burnout is respecting phases of lower training stress. These do not need to be complete breaks from running, but they should involve reduced volume, less structured intensity, and more freedom in how runs are performed. These periods allow fatigue to fully dissipate, minor aches to settle, and motivation to recharge. Many runners find that after even one or two easier weeks, training feels smoother and more enjoyable again.

Mental fatigue deserves as much attention as physical fatigue. Training that feels monotonous, overly rigid, or constantly pressured by performance expectations can gradually drain motivation. Allowing occasional flexibility in weekly structure, changing routes, running with friends, or simply running without tracking pace can help restore enjoyment without compromising overall fitness.

Long-term improvement depends far more on what runners can sustain than on what they can tolerate briefly. Programs that demand constant high intensity may look impressive on paper but rarely survive contact with real life. Missed sessions, lingering soreness, and declining enthusiasm eventually undermine consistency, which is the true driver of progress.

One of the most powerful aspects of the Norwegian-style approach is that it does not require heroic effort to produce results. Controlled threshold work, easy aerobic running, and gradual progression create fitness that accumulates quietly over time. Because sessions are repeatable, runners are able to train more weeks per year without interruption, which ultimately matters more than any single breakthrough workout.

Building year-round fitness also means accepting that not every month will produce visible performance gains. Some periods focus on strengthening foundations that only reveal themselves later when racing resumes. Trusting this process reduces the urge to constantly test fitness and allows training to serve development rather than short-term validation.

In practical terms, many runners benefit from limiting true race-focused periods to two or three times per year, each lasting several weeks, with longer stretches devoted to general aerobic development in between. This rhythm allows fitness to climb gradually while keeping motivation high and injury risk low.

The goal is not to avoid racing, but to place racing within a broader structure that supports continuous growth. When runners stop treating every workout as a test and every month as a peak, training becomes more sustainable, more enjoyable, and ultimately more effective.

Building fitness that lasts requires patience, restraint, and trust in simple principles repeated consistently. When training supports life rather than competing with it, runners are far more likely to stay healthy, motivated, and improving year after year instead of burning out after a few intense seasons.

# THIRTY-THREE

# When to Push and When to Protect Consistency

Knowing when to push training and when to back off is one of the most important skills a runner can develop. Many setbacks don't come from a single bad workout, but from repeatedly ignoring early signs of fatigue and continuing to add stress when the body is already struggling to recover. Protecting consistency often requires doing slightly less in the short term so that more can be done over the long term.

Productive training stress feels challenging but manageable. Runners should finish quality sessions feeling worked but not depleted, and should be able to approach the next key workout with stable pacing and reasonable energy. When training is in the right zone, fatigue rises and falls in predictable cycles, and easier days actually feel easy.

Problems usually start when fatigue becomes constant rather than temporary. When easy runs begin to feel heavy, sleep quality declines, motivation drops, or minor aches linger longer than usual, these are often signals that training load has exceeded current recovery capacity. At this point, pushing harder rarely produces better results. More often, it leads to forced breaks later.

One of the most common mistakes runners make is trying to "train through" fatigue in the hope that fitness will suddenly improve. While short periods of tiredness are normal during training blocks, prolonged fatigue almost always reduces workout quality, increases injury risk, and ultimately slows progress. Protecting training rhythm is far more valuable than completing one more hard session when the body is already under strain.

Small adjustments made early can prevent much bigger problems later. Reducing threshold volume for a week, shortening long runs slightly, or replacing one quality session with easy running can often restore balance quickly. These changes rarely cause meaningful fitness loss, but they often prevent weeks or months of disrupted training.

It's also important to recognize that not all tired days require action. Occasional sluggish runs after poor sleep or a stressful day are normal. What matters is whether those feelings persist and begin affecting multiple sessions. Patterns over time are far more informative than isolated bad workouts.

Good decision-making also means understanding that more training is not always better training. Adding frequency, volume, or intensity only helps when recovery can keep up. When recovery falls behind, performance gains slow down even if total workload continues to rise. Sustainable progression comes from matching training stress to current capacity, not from chasing theoretical "ideal" volumes.

Psychological factors also influence when to push and when to protect. Some runners struggle to back off even when they know they should, fearing they will lose fitness or fall behind. In reality, short recovery adjustments often lead to better training in the following weeks, not worse. Trusting this process becomes easier once runners experience how quickly form can rebound when fatigue is allowed to drop.

Another helpful guideline is to judge training by the quality of key sessions rather than by weekly totals. If threshold sessions remain controlled, long runs feel manageable, and easy days restore energy, training is likely on track. When quality sessions start to deteriorate, that is often the first sign that adjustments are needed.

Protecting consistency also means being flexible when life adds extra stress. Work deadlines, travel, illness, or family demands all reduce recovery capacity even if running volume stays the same. During these periods, maintaining training structure with slightly reduced volume or intensity is usually more effective than forcing full workloads that the body cannot absorb.

Pushing at the right time is still important. Training must be challenging enough to stimulate adaptation. However, productive pushing happens when the body is prepared, not when it's already overloaded. The goal is to apply stress in doses that can be repeated week after week, not in bursts that require extended recovery.

Ultimately, the strongest runners are not the ones who train the hardest on their best days, but the ones who manage their worst days wisely. Knowing when to push and when to protect is what allows training to continue uninterrupted, and uninterrupted training is what drives lasting performance gains.

# THIRTY-FOUR

# Strength Training That Supports Running

Strength training is often misunderstood in running programs. Some runners avoid it entirely, worried it will make them heavy or sore, while others add long gym sessions that leave them too fatigued to run well. The Norwegian approach takes a different view. Strength work is not meant to build muscle for appearance or to replace running. Its role is to support efficient movement, protect joints and tendons, and help the body tolerate consistent training over long periods of time. When done correctly, strength training should feel simple, controlled, and sustainable. It should make running feel more stable and resilient, not harder to recover from.

Running is a highly repetitive activity. Each step places similar forces through the same tissues thousands of times per session. While this repetition is excellent for developing aerobic fitness, it does not fully strengthen the muscles responsible for stability, balance, and force control. Over time, small weaknesses can develop in areas like the hips, calves, feet, and trunk (the muscles of your midsection, including the abdominals, lower back, and muscles around the spine). These weaknesses don't always cause immediate injury, but they increase strain on tendons and joints and make it harder to maintain good mechanics as fatigue builds.

Strength training helps fill these gaps. It improves how forces are absorbed and transferred through the body, making each stride slightly more efficient and less stressful. This becomes especially important late in long runs and races, when form tends to deteriorate and injury risk increases. The goal is not to run differently, but to give the body the strength it needs to keep running the same way even when tired.

Elite runners using Norwegian-style systems do not rely on heavy lifting or exhausting gym sessions. In fact, many keep strength work deliberately minimal. Their priority is always the quality of running sessions, not how much weight they can move. Strength work is used as insurance. It protects their ability to train consistently, absorb higher volumes of threshold work, and stay healthy across long seasons rather than peaking briefly and breaking down.

For recreational runners, this principle matters even more. Most runners have limited time, variable recovery, and additional stress from work and daily life. Strength work that is too demanding quickly competes with running and undermines the very consistency it is meant to support. Short, simple sessions performed regularly are far more effective than complex routines that are difficult to maintain.

For most runners, two short strength sessions per week are enough to see meaningful benefits. Each session should last about fifteen to twenty-five minutes and leave you feeling stable and activated rather than exhausted. If legs feel heavy, coordination feels off, or running quality drops after strength work, volume should be reduced. Strength training should never make you dread your next run.

These sessions fit best after easy runs or on non-running days. Placing strength work after easy running allows enough recovery before threshold sessions and long runs, which should always remain the priority. As training intensity increases or race day approaches, strength sessions should become shorter and lighter, shifting toward maintenance rather than progression.

## 25-Minute Strength Session (No Equipment)

This session uses simple supersets to save time and limit fatigue. You'll perform two exercises back-to-back, rest briefly, then repeat once more before moving on. Rest about 30–45 seconds between supersets.

**Lower Body and Stability**

Split Squats: $2 \times 10$ per leg

Single-Leg Calf Raises: $2 \times 15$ per leg

So do one set of 10 split squats on each leg, followed immediately by 15 single-leg calf raises on each leg. Take about 45 seconds of rest, then repeat the same two exercises once more. When finished, move on to the next pair below.

**Hip and Glute Control**

Single-Leg Glute Bridges: $2 \times 12$ per leg

Side Leg Raises (or Standing Hip Abductions): $2 \times 12$–$15$ per side

**Trunk Stability (core muscles of the abdomen and lower back)**

Plank: $2 \times 30$–$45$ seconds

Bird Dogs: $2 \times 8$–$10$ slow reps per side

**Upper Body Support**

Push-Ups: $2 \times 10$–$15$

Bodyweight Rows (bench, railing, or table edge): $2 \times 8$–$12$

The total time should be approximately 22–25 minutes. You should finish feeling stable and switched on, not exhausted. If this session makes your next run feel heavy, reduce reps slightly rather than skipping strength work entirely.

# 15-Minute Quick Strength Session (No Equipment)

This shortened session keeps the most important movements and uses simple supersets to maintain strength and stability when time is limited. Perform each pair back-to-back, rest briefly, then repeat once more before moving on.

**Lower Body and Stability**

Split Squats: 2 × 10 per leg

Single-Leg Calf Raises: 2 × 15 per leg

So do one set of 10 split squats on each leg, followed immediately by 15 single-leg calf raises on each leg. Rest about 45 seconds, then repeat the same two exercises once more before moving to the next pair.

Time: ~5–6 minutes

**Hip and Trunk Stability** (core muscles of the abdomen and lower back)

Single-Leg Glute Bridges: 2 × 12 per leg

Plank: 2 × 30–45 seconds

Perform one set of single-leg glute bridges on each leg, followed immediately by a plank hold. Rest briefly, then repeat once more before moving on.

Time: ~5 minutes

**Upper Body Support**

Push-Ups: 2 × 10–15

Bodyweight Rows (bench, railing, or table edge): 2 × 8–12

Perform push-ups followed immediately by bodyweight rows. Rest about 30–45 seconds, then repeat once more.

Time: ~3–4 minutes

The total time should be approximately 12–15 minutes. This session works best after easy runs or on rest days and is ideal during busy weeks, travel, or late-race preparation. You should finish feeling activated and stable, not fatigued. If running quality begins to suffer, reduce reps slightly rather than removing strength work altogether.

# THIRTY-FIVE

# The Recovery Tool That Makes Training Work

Most runners think improvement comes from running more miles or pushing harder workouts. While training is essential, it only creates the stimulus for improvement. The actual fitness gains happen later, during recovery, and sleep is the most powerful recovery tool the body has. Without enough high-quality sleep, even the best-designed training plan cannot produce its full benefits. In simple terms, training breaks the body down slightly, and sleep is when it gets built back stronger.

Threshold sessions and long runs place meaningful stress on the aerobic system, muscles, and connective tissue. This stress is necessary for adaptation, but only if the body is given enough time and resources to respond. During sleep, the body releases hormones that repair muscle tissue, strengthen tendons, restore energy stores, and rebalance the nervous system. When sleep is short or fragmented, these recovery processes are blunted. The same workout that should make you fitter instead becomes harder to absorb, leaving you feeling flat, sore, or unusually tired in the following days.

This is why poor sleep often leads to a weaker response to the same training. Two runners can follow identical plans, but the one who sleeps better will usually improve more, recover faster, and tolerate higher-quality sessions more consistently. Over time, this difference compounds. The better-slept runner builds fitness steadily, while the sleep-deprived runner starts skipping sessions, cutting workouts short, or feeling like every run takes more effort than it should.

Consistency is what ultimately drives long-term progress, and recovery is what protects consistency. Most training setbacks do not come from a single hard workout, but from accumulated fatigue that slowly chips away at motivation, performance, and physical resilience. Missed sleep leads to slower recovery, slower recovery leads to lingering soreness and mental burnout, and those eventually lead to missed training days. When recovery improves, consistency improves, and when consistency improves, fitness almost always follows.

For this reason, sleep should be viewed as part of training, not something separate from it. Just as easy runs support threshold sessions and long runs support race endurance, sleep supports every adaptation your training is trying to create. It does not replace training, but it determines how much benefit you actually get from the work you put in.

## What Actually Happens During Sleep Cycles

Sleep is not one long, uniform state of rest. Across the night, the body moves through repeating sleep cycles, each lasting roughly ninety minutes. Within each cycle, you pass through light sleep, deep sleep, and REM sleep. These stages appear in different proportions as the night goes on, and each plays a distinct role in how the body and brain recover from training.

Light sleep is the entry point into each cycle. Heart rate slows, breathing becomes more regular, and muscle tension begins to drop. While this stage does not drive major physical repair, it prepares the nervous system to transition into deeper, more restorative sleep. Without enough light sleep, the body struggles to access deep and REM stages consistently.

Deep sleep, also known as slow-wave sleep, is where most physical recovery takes place. During this stage, growth hormone release increases, supporting muscle repair, tissue rebuilding, and bone strengthening. Blood flow is directed toward muscles and connective tissue, inflammation from training begins to settle, and the immune system is reinforced. This is when the body actually adapts to the stress created by threshold sessions, long runs, and strength work.

When deep sleep is shortened or fragmented, recovery falls behind. Muscle repair is incomplete, small amounts of training damage accumulate, and soreness lingers longer than it should. Many runners who feel constantly tired despite following a sensible plan are not under-training, they are under-recovering.

REM sleep, which stands for rapid eye movement sleep, is where most neurological recovery occurs. This stage supports coordination, rhythm, pacing awareness, and motor learning. The brain processes the movements and effort patterns practiced during the day and refines them into smoother, more automatic skills. REM sleep also plays a key role in emotional regulation and focus, both of which affect how runners handle discomfort and decision-making during races.

For runners, this means REM sleep is not just about memory. When REM sleep is reduced, coordination subtly worsens, reaction time slows, and pacing becomes less stable, especially late in races when fatigue is high. This is one reason runners may feel physically capable but mentally flat after poor sleep.

Across a full night, the body needs multiple complete sleep cycles to accumulate enough deep and REM sleep. Early cycles tend to contain more deep sleep, while later cycles contain more REM sleep. When sleep is cut short, the later cycles are most often missed, which disproportionately affects mental sharpness, pacing control, and emotional resilience.

This is also why time in bed is not the same as quality sleep. Frequent awakenings, scrolling on a phone, or falling asleep with the television on can fragment sleep and prevent the body from staying in deep or REM stages long enough to complete the recovery process. Even if total hours look reasonable, recovery can still be incomplete.

Sleep cycles work much like training intervals. You would not stop a threshold session halfway through and expect the same benefit. In the same way, interrupting sleep cycles or consistently cutting sleep short reduces the recovery effect, even if effort and training quality are otherwise high.

Training load increases sleep needs. Long runs, threshold sessions, and strength work all place additional stress on muscles and the nervous system, which raises the amount of deep and REM sleep required for full recovery. During heavier training weeks, many runners need closer to eight to ten hours of sleep rather than the minimum seven often recommended for general health.

Protecting sleep is not about being lazy or fragile. It is about allowing training to actually produce the adaptations it is designed to create. When sleep cycles are protected, recovery becomes more complete, pacing becomes more stable, and training adaptations accumulate smoothly instead of being blunted by fatigue.

## Creating the Ideal Sleep Environment (Your Modern "Cave")

For most of human history, sleep happened in very simple conditions. People slept in dark, quiet, cool shelters, often caves or enclosed spaces that protected them from predators and weather. There were no glowing screens, no streetlights, and no artificial brightness stretching late into the night. The only light after sunset came from fire, which produces warm, low-intensity light that does not strongly interfere with the body's sleep signals. Over thousands of years, the human nervous system evolved to associate darkness, quiet, and falling temperatures with safety and rest.

That biology has not changed just because modern bedrooms look different. Your brain still relies on the same cues to know when it is time to sleep. When light levels drop, the brain releases melatonin, the hormone that makes you feel sleepy and tells your body to shift into recovery mode. When the environment is cool and still, your nervous system relaxes and deeper stages of sleep become easier to reach. When those cues are missing, falling asleep becomes harder and sleep tends to be lighter and more fragmented.

This is why sleep experts often recommend creating a modern version of a "sleep cave." That doesn't mean changing your entire lifestyle, but it does mean paying attention to a few key factors that strongly influence sleep quality.

Darkness is the most important. Even small sources of light can reduce melatonin production and keep the brain in a more alert state. This includes light from streetlamps, hallway lights, TV screens, chargers, digital clocks, and notification LEDs. Ideally, the room should be dark enough that you cannot easily see your hand in front of your face. Blackout curtains are one option, but they aren't required. Covering windows with thick curtains, towels, or dark fabric can block a surprising amount of light. Any glowing electronics should be turned off or covered. If something cannot be switched off, placing a T-shirt or tape over the light is often enough to remove the stimulus.

Temperature is the next major factor. To fall asleep and stay asleep, the body needs to lower its core temperature slightly. A cooler room supports this natural drop and helps the body move into deeper stages of sleep. Most people sleep best in a room that feels slightly cool rather than warm. Opening a window, using a fan, or lowering the thermostat can all help. Fans also provide gentle background noise, which can reduce sleep disruptions from traffic, voices, or household sounds.

Quiet is helpful, but complete silence is not always necessary. What matters most is consistency. Sudden or unpredictable noises are more disruptive than steady background sound. If your environment is noisy, white noise from a fan or a simple noise app can help mask sharp sounds and reduce nighttime awakenings. Earplugs can also be useful, especially during travel or in shared living spaces.

Comfort also matters, but not in the way most people think. The goal is not luxury, but support. A mattress that keeps the spine in a neutral position and pillows that support the neck without forcing it forward or sideways help reduce muscle tension during sleep. Bedding should allow heat to escape rather than trapping warmth. Heavy blankets that cause overheating can quietly disrupt sleep even if you do not fully wake up.

Finally, the bedroom should be associated with sleep, not stimulation. Watching videos, scrolling on social media, or doing stressful work in bed trains the brain to associate that space with alertness rather than rest. Over time, this makes it harder to fall asleep quickly. Using the bed mainly for sleep helps strengthen the mental connection between lying down and switching off.

None of these changes are extreme, expensive, or complicated, but together they create an environment that supports the body's natural recovery systems. When runners train hard, small improvements in sleep quality can have a large impact on how well they absorb that training. Creating the right environment does not replace discipline or effort, but it makes the results of that effort far more reliable.

**Light, Screens, and Why Your Brain Still Thinks It's Daytime**

Your brain does not know what time it is by looking at a clock. It decides whether it should be awake or asleep based almost entirely on light exposure. For most of human history, this system worked very simply. Bright light during the day meant it was time to be alert and active. Darkness after sunset meant it was time to slow down and recover. Modern lighting and screens have disrupted that signal in ways our biology has not had time to adapt to.

The biggest issue is not just brightness, but the type of light. Phones, tablets, TVs, and computer screens emit a large amount of blue light. Blue light is especially powerful at suppressing melatonin, the hormone that tells your body it is time to sleep. When melatonin is blocked, your body may feel physically tired, but your brain remains in a more alert state. This makes it harder to fall asleep and reduces the amount of deep and **REM** sleep you get, even if you manage to sleep for the same number of hours.

This is why many people say they feel exhausted but still cannot fall asleep. The body wants rest, but the brain is receiving signals that it is still daytime. Scrolling through social media, watching videos, or responding to messages late at night keeps the nervous system stimulated and delays the natural transition into recovery mode.

Even small amounts of screen exposure can have an effect. A few minutes of bright light can push melatonin release back by thirty minutes or more. When this happens night after night, sleep schedules drift later, and total sleep time gradually shrinks, even if you are still getting into bed at roughly the same time.

Televisions create a similar problem, especially when watched in dark rooms. The contrast between the bright screen and dark surroundings makes the light feel even more intense to the brain. Falling asleep with the TV on may seem relaxing, but it often leads to lighter sleep and more nighttime awakenings.

One simple but powerful habit is setting a consistent screen cutoff time. This does not need to be extreme. Even turning off bright screens thirty to sixty minutes before bed can significantly improve sleep quality. During that time, lighting in the home should also be dimmed if possible. Warm, low-level lighting is far less disruptive than bright white overhead lights.

Many devices offer night mode or blue-light filtering settings that shift the screen toward warmer colors in the evening. These features are better than nothing and can reduce some of the negative impact of screens, but they don't fully solve the problem. Bright light and mental stimulation still keep the brain alert, even if the color temperature is slightly warmer. These settings should be seen as damage control, not a replacement for reducing screen use before bed.

It's also important to think about the first and last light your eyes see each day. Getting natural daylight early in the morning helps anchor your internal clock and makes it easier to feel sleepy at night. In contrast, exposing your eyes to bright screens late at night shifts that clock later and later. This is one of the reasons many people feel wired at night and groggy in the morning even when they think they are getting enough sleep.

For runners trying to recover from threshold workouts and long runs, this matters more than it seems. Reduced sleep quality affects muscle repair, hormone balance, immune function, and mental focus. Over time, that translates into slower adaptation to training and higher risk of burnout or injury. Cutting down on late-night screen use is one of the simplest ways to improve recovery without changing anything about the training itself.

The goal is not perfection, but consistency. You do not need to avoid screens forever, but creating a regular window before bed where your brain is not flooded with artificial daylight makes it far easier to fall asleep quickly and stay asleep deeply.

## Bedtime Routines That Actually Improve Sleep Quality

Falling asleep isn't something you can force. It happens when the nervous system shifts from an alert, protective state into a relaxed, recovery-focused state. This shift doesn't happen instantly the moment you lie down. It's something the body moves into gradually, and your habits in the final hour before bed play a huge role in how smoothly that transition happens.

Many runners struggle with sleep not because they are not tired, but because their brain is still switched on. Training stress, work stress, social stimulation, and screen use all keep the nervous system in a heightened state. A simple wind-down routine helps tell your body that the day is ending and that it is safe to rest.

One of the most effective tools is controlled breathing. Slow breathing patterns stimulate the parasympathetic nervous system, which is responsible for rest and recovery. A simple method is box breathing. Inhale for four seconds, hold for four seconds, exhale for four seconds, and hold again for four seconds before the next breath. Repeating this for two to five minutes can noticeably lower heart rate and muscle tension. The goal is not perfect technique, but steady rhythm and relaxed breathing.

Another powerful habit is journaling. When your mind is busy, your brain keeps replaying tasks, worries, and plans because it's trying to make sure nothing gets forgotten. Writing these thoughts down signals to your brain that it no longer needs to hold onto them. This can be as simple as listing what you did that day, what you need to do tomorrow, and how you felt during training. For runners, this is also a perfect time to note how a workout felt, what pace felt controlled, and whether recovery seems on track. Over time, this becomes both a sleep tool and a training log.

Reading is another effective way to calm the mind, especially when it replaces screen time. Physical books or e-readers without bright backlighting are best. The goal is to keep the brain lightly engaged without emotional or visual stimulation. Fast-paced shows, social media, and intense news stories tend to have the opposite effect and keep the brain alert even when the body is tired.

Consistency matters as much as the activities themselves. Going through the same few steps each night teaches your brain to associate that routine with sleep. Over time, your body begins to wind down automatically when the routine starts, making it easier to fall asleep without effort.

Bedtime itself should also be reasonably consistent. Going to sleep and waking up at similar times each day helps regulate your internal clock, which controls when melatonin rises and when alertness naturally drops. Large swings in bedtime, especially between weekdays and weekends, confuse this rhythm and make it harder to fall asleep and wake up feeling rested.

It's tempting to think that you can catch up on sleep by sleeping in on off days, but this usually makes it harder to fall asleep the following night and starts a cycle of late nights and groggy mornings. A more reliable strategy is keeping sleep and wake times within roughly the same one-hour window every day, even when training schedules change.

Small changes in the evening routine often produce bigger improvements in sleep quality than people expect. Better sleep leads to better recovery, and better recovery allows threshold sessions and long runs to actually create adaptation instead of just accumulating fatigue. Over weeks and months, this is one of the quiet advantages that separates steady progress from constant frustration.

## Food, Timing, and Why Late Nights and Heavy Meals Disrupt Recovery

Sleep and nutrition are closely connected, especially for runners who are placing regular stress on their bodies through training. What you eat and when you eat does not just affect energy levels during the day. It also affects how easily you fall asleep, how deeply you sleep, and how well your body recovers overnight.

When you eat a large meal late at night, your body has to divert blood flow and energy toward digestion at the exact time it should be shifting into repair mode. Instead of focusing on muscle recovery, hormone regulation, and nervous system recovery, your body is still processing food. This can delay sleep onset, increase nighttime awakenings, and reduce the amount of deep sleep you get, even if you remain in bed for a full night.

Finishing your last substantial meal about two to three hours before bed gives your body enough time to complete most of the digestive work before sleep. This makes it easier to fall asleep and allows the recovery processes that happen during deep sleep to operate more efficiently. This timing becomes more important as training load increases, because the body needs uninterrupted recovery to adapt to threshold sessions and long runs.

Late-night sugar can also interfere with sleep in a less obvious way. Sugary foods cause a rapid rise in blood sugar, followed by a drop later in the night. That drop can trigger the release of stress hormones such as cortisol, which may partially wake you up even if you do not remember it. These brief awakenings fragment sleep and reduce time spent in deeper stages, which are the most important for physical recovery.

If you are hungry closer to bedtime, small and simple snacks are better than heavy meals. Protein-based options or foods that digest slowly are less likely to cause blood sugar swings. The goal is to avoid going to bed either overly full or uncomfortably hungry, both of which can disrupt sleep quality.

Caffeine is another major factor that affects sleep without always being obvious. Caffeine blocks adenosine, a chemical that helps your brain feel sleepy, and it remains in the body much longer than most people realize. Even if you can fall asleep after drinking caffeine late in the day, sleep quality is often reduced. Deep sleep in particular can be suppressed, which is exactly the stage that supports muscle repair and immune function.

For most runners, stopping caffeine intake by late morning or early afternoon leads to noticeably better sleep within a few days. Energy drinks and pre-workout supplements are especially important to monitor, as they often contain much higher doses of caffeine than coffee and may also include other stimulants that linger in the system.

Alcohol can also disrupt recovery, even though it may make you feel sleepy at first. Alcohol fragments sleep, reduces REM sleep, and increases nighttime awakenings. For runners, this means less neurological recovery, poorer coordination, and slower muscle repair. Even small amounts can have measurable effects on sleep quality.

Hydration plays a role as well. Going to bed dehydrated can increase muscle cramping and raise heart rate overnight, but drinking large amounts of fluid right before bed increases the chance of waking up to use the bathroom. Spreading fluid intake throughout the day and tapering slightly in the final hour before bed usually works best.

None of these habits require strict perfection to make a difference. Small shifts in meal timing, caffeine use, and evening snacks often lead to noticeable improvements in how rested you feel in the morning. Better sleep quality allows your body to absorb training more effectively, which is what ultimately turns workouts into long-term fitness rather than short-term fatigue.

## The Role of Naps in Training Recovery

Naps can be a helpful recovery tool for runners when used with intention. While they don't replace high-quality nighttime sleep, they can reduce accumulated fatigue, improve alertness, and support recovery during demanding training periods. Used well, naps can make training feel smoother and more manageable, especially during heavier weeks or after an occasional short night of sleep.

For most runners, short naps of around 20 to 30 minutes work best. These brief naps refresh the brain and nervous system without dropping into deep sleep. Because deep sleep takes longer to reach, keeping naps short helps avoid the groggy, sluggish feeling known as sleep inertia. After a short nap, runners usually wake up feeling clearer, more focused, and physically lighter, without affecting their ability to fall asleep later that night.

You may have heard the idea of a "27-minute nap." This comes from NASA research conducted on pilots and astronauts, which found that a nap of about 26–27 minutes significantly improved alertness and performance while minimizing grogginess. While this research wasn't specific to runners, the principle translates well: short naps that stop before deep sleep tend to provide the biggest benefit with the least downside.

Longer naps, typically 60 to 90 minutes, allow the body to move through a full sleep cycle, including deep and REM sleep. These can be useful during periods of very heavy training, travel across time zones, or major sleep disruption. When used occasionally, they can support recovery and mental reset. However, because longer naps reduce sleep pressure, they work best as occasional tools rather than daily habits.

Timing matters as much as duration. Early afternoon, usually between 1:00 and 3:00 p.m., is ideal. This aligns with a natural dip in alertness driven by circadian rhythms. Napping later in the day, especially in the early evening, often makes it harder to fall asleep at night and can reduce overall sleep quality.

Naps tend to be most helpful during heavy training blocks, after long runs or threshold sessions, or when training volume is increasing. In these situations, a short nap can support recovery enough to preserve workout quality without changing the overall training plan.

If naps start to feel necessary every single day just to get through normal training, that's usually a signal to look at nighttime sleep first. Improving sleep duration, consistency, and environment almost always produces greater benefits than relying on daytime sleep alone. When nighttime sleep is solid, naps become a bonus rather than a necessity.

Used intentionally, naps are a simple way to smooth out training stress, improve mental sharpness, and protect consistency during demanding phases. The foundation of recovery will always be nighttime sleep, but naps can work alongside it as a practical, flexible tool that helps runners absorb training more effectively over time.

**Sleep During Travel, Races, and Hotels**

Travel, competitions, and race weekends often create the worst sleep of an athlete's entire training cycle, even though these are the moments when recovery matters most. New environments, unfamiliar beds, noise, schedule changes, and pre-race nerves can all interfere with normal sleep patterns. While perfect sleep isn't always possible on the road, small adjustments can protect recovery enough to prevent performance from slipping.

The goal when traveling is to recreate your usual sleep environment as closely as possible. That means aiming for the same basic conditions as at home: dark, quiet, and cool. An eye mask can block out hotel hallway lights, street lamps, or early morning sunlight. Earplugs or white noise from a phone or small speaker can reduce sudden noises like doors closing or people moving in nearby rooms. If the room feels warm, adjusting the air conditioning or using a fan helps keep body temperature lower, which supports deeper sleep. These tools are simple, inexpensive, and easy to pack, but they can make a major difference in how rested you feel the next day.

Adrenaline is another major sleep disruptor during races and tournaments. After intense competition or even just the anticipation of a big event, the nervous system often stays in a heightened state, making it difficult to relax and fall asleep. Instead of lying in bed replaying the race or worrying about the next day, it helps to use the same calming routines that work at home. Slow breathing, light stretching, journaling, or reading can help shift the body out of high alert mode and back toward recovery. The goal isn't to force sleep but to create conditions where sleep can happen naturally once the body settles.

Food and caffeine choices become even more important during travel and race weekends. Late-night energy drinks, coffee, sugary snacks, or heavy meals can easily delay sleep or reduce sleep quality. While it may feel tempting to use caffeine to stay alert between events, especially during long tournament days, it often comes at the cost of poor sleep that night. Whenever possible, caffeine should be limited to earlier in the day, and evening meals should be kept lighter and lower in sugar. Hydration remains important, but excessive fluid intake right before bed can also increase nighttime bathroom trips and disrupt sleep cycles.

It's also helpful to accept that sleep on race weekends may not be perfect, and that's normal. One slightly restless night will not ruin performance if overall training and recovery have been strong. What matters more is protecting the habits that keep sleep as stable as possible rather than adding new stress by worrying about every lost minute. Staying calm about sleep often leads to better sleep than trying to control it too aggressively.

When athletes prepare for sleep the same way they prepare for competition, recovery becomes portable. With a few simple tools and consistent habits, it is possible to protect enough rest to support performance even in unfamiliar environments. That ability to recover anywhere becomes a quiet advantage, especially during demanding race periods when others begin to accumulate fatigue.

# THIRTY-SIX

# Fueling the Training You're Doing

Nutrition does not need to be extreme, restrictive, or complicated to support strong running performance. The goal is not perfect eating, but consistent fueling that allows training to be absorbed, repeated, and progressed over time. In the same way the Norwegian method removes unnecessary intensity from training, it also removes unnecessary complexity from nutrition.

At its core, performance nutrition is about three things: having enough energy to train well, providing the body with the raw materials to recover, and timing intake so those processes happen reliably. When these basics are covered, most runners feel better, recover faster, and stop fighting low energy or inconsistent training weeks.

Rather than focusing on trends, hacks, or rigid rules, this chapter centers on the nutritional principles that consistently support threshold training, long runs, and repeatable weeks. The priority is not dieting for appearance, but fueling for performance.

## Carbohydrates as the Primary Fuel

Carbohydrates are the main fuel source for running, especially when training includes threshold work, steady aerobic efforts, and long runs. These sessions rely heavily on stored muscle glycogen, which is derived from the carbohydrates you eat. When glycogen availability is high, training feels more controlled, paces are easier to sustain, and recovery between sessions improves. When glycogen is low, even moderate workouts can feel unusually hard.

This is why carbohydrate intake is so closely linked to training quality. Runners who consistently underfuel with carbohydrates often describe threshold sessions as "heavy," "flat," or harder than expected for the pace. The effort feels high not because fitness is lacking, but because the body is short on its preferred fuel. Over time, this leads to compromised workouts, reduced progression, and increased fatigue across the week.

Carbohydrates support both the aerobic and glycolytic energy systems that dominate 10K, half marathon, and threshold-focused training. They allow you to hold steady paces without drifting, maintain form late in long runs, and recover more quickly so quality sessions can be repeated. This is one of the reasons Norwegian-style programs emphasize fueling alongside training rather than treating nutrition as an afterthought.

The type of carbohydrate matters less than consistency and timing. Whole food sources such as rice, potatoes, oats, pasta, fruit, and bread all provide effective fuel when eaten regularly. Highly processed carbohydrates are not inherently bad, but they should serve a purpose, such as quick energy before or after hard sessions, rather than forming the base of every meal.

## Energy Intake, Calorie Burn, and Why Most Runners Underfuel

One of the most common problems among runners is not training too hard, but eating too little to support the training they are doing. This often happens unintentionally. Runners add mileage or intensity, but food intake stays roughly the same, slowly creating an energy deficit that shows up as flat workouts, poor recovery, and unstable pacing.

A simple rule of thumb helps put running energy cost into perspective. Most runners burn about 90–110 calories per mile, regardless of pace. This means the faster runner finishes the mile sooner, but the energy cost is similar. For many recreational runners, that works out to roughly 80–120 calories per 10 minutes of running, depending on body weight and pace. A lighter runner at an easy pace will be toward the lower end, while a heavier runner or faster pace will be toward the higher end.

When this adds up over the week, the numbers become significant. A runner training six days per week with a mix of easy runs, threshold sessions, and a long run may easily burn 2,000–3,000 calories per week from running alone, before accounting for daily movement, strength work, or sport-specific training. If those calories are not replaced, the body adapts by reducing recovery capacity, increasing fatigue, and raising stress hormones, all of which interfere with threshold training quality.

This is why carb availability is so closely linked to training quality. Threshold work depends on stable energy supply. When runners underfuel, the same pace produces higher effort, breathing becomes less controlled, and lactate accumulates sooner. Over time, this breaks the repeatability that the Norwegian method relies on.

One practical tool for gaining awareness is tracking food intake for a short period, not to micromanage nutrition forever, but to calibrate reality. Using an app like MyFitnessPal for one normal training week can be very helpful. The goal is not perfection and not long-term tracking. The goal is simply to answer two questions:

• Roughly how many calories am I eating?

• Does that match the workload I am asking my body to handle?

Many runners are surprised to find they are several hundred calories short each day, especially on long run days. Once that gap is visible, it becomes much easier to adjust portions, add carbohydrates around training, or include an extra snack without guessing.

In the Norwegian approach, nutrition is not about restriction or precision dieting. It is about supporting the work. When calories and carbohydrates are sufficient, threshold sessions feel controlled, long runs remain steady, and fitness builds predictably over time. When energy intake is too low, even well-designed training plans struggle to produce results.

## Protein for Recovery, Not Bulking

For runners, total daily protein intake matters most. If you are not consistently eating enough protein across the day, timing and distribution won't fix the problem. Recovery depends first on hitting an adequate daily amount, especially when training includes threshold work, long runs, and strength sessions.

Once total intake is consistently covered, spreading protein across the day becomes the next layer of optimization. Dividing protein into doses of roughly 25–30 grams every three to four hours helps keep muscle repair and connective tissue recovery active throughout the day. This improves day-to-day recovery and supports the ability to repeat quality sessions week after week.

Protein's role in a distance runner's program is repair and resilience, not muscle size. Running creates small amounts of muscle damage and connective tissue stress. Protein supplies the amino acids needed to repair that damage, reinforce tendons and muscles, and allow adaptation to occur between sessions. Without enough protein overall, soreness lingers, fatigue accumulates faster, and training becomes harder to absorb.

Post-training intake matters, but it does not need to be complicated. Consuming protein within one to two hours after harder sessions helps initiate recovery, especially when paired with carbohydrates. This supports both muscle repair and glycogen replenishment. However, this only works well if total daily intake is already sufficient.

More protein is not always better. Extremely high protein intake does not replace carbohydrates, does not speed recovery indefinitely, and does not compensate for underfueling. Once needs are met, consistency matters far more than excess.

When protein intake is adequate and consistent, runners tend to recover faster between sessions, experience fewer lingering aches, and feel more stable across training weeks. This reliability is exactly what allows structured training systems like the Norwegian method to work long term.

## Daily Protein Needs for Runners

A practical guideline for endurance athletes is 0.7–0.8 grams of protein per pound of body weight (or 1.6–1.8 grams per kilogram) per day during regular training.

Once this total is reliably met, splitting intake into three to five servings of ~25–30 grams across the day is an effective way to support recovery without overthinking it.

| Body Weight | Daily Protein Target |
| --- | --- |
| 110 lbs (50 kg) | 80–90 g |
| 132 lbs (60 kg) | 95–110 g |
| 154 lbs (70 kg) | 110–125 g |
| 176 lbs (80 kg) | 125–140 g |
| 198 lbs (90 kg) | 140–160 g |
| 220 lbs (100 kg) | 155–175 g |

## Hydration as Performance-Critical

Hydration isn't just about comfort or avoiding cramps. For runners, hydration directly affects pace control, heart rate, coordination, and recovery. Even mild dehydration can make easy runs feel harder, threshold sessions feel unstable, and long runs feel disproportionately draining. When hydration is off, training quality drops long before you feel truly thirsty.

A useful starting point is sweat rate awareness. Runners vary widely in how much fluid they lose, even at the same pace and in the same conditions. Body size, pace, heat, humidity, and clothing all influence sweat loss. Some runners lose less than about 17 oz per hour (500 ml), while others can lose over 68 oz per hour (2 liters) in warm conditions. Knowing where you fall on that spectrum helps you hydrate with intention rather than guessing.

A simple way to estimate sweat rate is to weigh yourself before and after a run, accounting for any fluids consumed during the session. Roughly, 2.2 lb (1 kg) of body weight lost equals about 34 oz (1 liter) of fluid. This does not need to be done often. One or two measurements in different conditions is enough to give you a useful baseline.

Hydration needs increase during longer sessions and harder workouts, especially threshold runs and long runs. These sessions place higher demands on blood volume, temperature regulation, and muscle function. Starting these workouts slightly dehydrated almost always leads to poorer pacing and earlier fatigue, even if total weekly mileage is reasonable.

Sodium becomes increasingly important as duration and heat increase. Sweat contains not just water, but electrolytes, especially sodium. Replacing fluid without replacing sodium can dilute blood sodium levels and reduce fluid absorption, which is why simply drinking large amounts of plain water during long or hot runs sometimes makes runners feel worse rather than better.

For most runners, plain water is sufficient for runs under 60 minutes in cool conditions. For longer sessions, hot weather, or heavy sweaters, adding sodium improves hydration effectiveness and helps maintain performance. This can come from sports drinks, electrolyte mixes, or simple salted foods consumed around training. You do not need extreme sodium intake, just enough to support fluid retention and absorption.

Hydration also affects recovery. Starting the day dehydrated or finishing sessions underhydrated slows glycogen replenishment, increases perceived soreness, and raises heart rate the following day. Consistently good hydration supports steadier training weeks and reduces the chance that fatigue quietly accumulates.

The goal isn't perfect hydration at every moment, but stable hydration across the day. Drinking regularly, paying attention to urine color, and adjusting intake based on conditions is usually enough. When hydration is treated as performance-critical rather than an afterthought, training becomes more predictable and easier to repeat, which is exactly what structured systems like the Norwegian approach rely on.

**Consistency Over Hacks**

Long-term performance is built far more by what you do most days than by occasional "perfect" days. In nutrition, this means consistency beats complexity every time. Runners who eat roughly the same types of meals, at similar times each day, tend to fuel training better than those who constantly experiment with new diets, timing tricks, or restrictive rules.

One of the biggest hidden benefits of consistency is low decision fatigue. When you already know what breakfast, lunch, and post-run meals look like, you are far less likely to underfuel or skip recovery nutrition simply because you are tired or busy. This is especially important during heavier training weeks, when both physical and mental energy are already taxed.

Consistent meals also stabilize energy levels. Eating similar amounts of carbohydrates and protein each day helps maintain glycogen stores, reduces large swings in hunger, and makes training paces feel more predictable. When fueling is steady, it becomes easier to interpret training feedback. A bad workout is more likely to reflect fatigue or recovery needs rather than random nutrition errors.

This does not mean eating the exact same foods forever. Variety can still exist within a stable structure. What matters is that the overall pattern stays reliable. Runners following structured training systems benefit most when nutrition supports repeatability rather than chasing novelty.

If a nutrition strategy requires constant tracking, frequent willpower, or daily motivation, it is unlikely to hold up over months of training. The best nutrition plan is the one you can execute calmly, even on busy or stressful days. When nutrition feels boring but dependable, it is usually working exactly as intended.

**Food First, Supplements Second**

Supplements are often marketed as shortcuts to performance, but for runners, their impact is small compared to solid daily nutrition. Training quality, recovery, and consistency are driven primarily by adequate calories, sufficient carbohydrates, enough protein, and proper hydration. Supplements can support these foundations, but they cannot replace them.

Among the many supplements available, creatine and caffeine are the only two that consistently show meaningful performance benefits for most athletes. Creatine can support strength, repeated high-intensity efforts, and muscle recovery, while caffeine can improve alertness, perceived effort, and pacing control when used strategically. Even these should be used with intention rather than automatically.

Most other supplements provide minimal benefit if basic nutrition is already in place. Products like BCAAs, fat burners, detoxes, and many "recovery" blends are often redundant or unnecessary when protein intake and overall calorie intake are sufficient. In some cases, they distract runners from addressing the real issue, which is underfueling or poor recovery habits.

The supplement industry also carries risks. Products are not tightly regulated, and contamination or inaccurate labeling does occur. For competitive athletes, this can carry serious consequences. Even for recreational runners, relying heavily on supplements can create a false sense of security while foundational habits remain inconsistent.

A simple rule works well: fix food first. If training feels flat, recovery is poor, or energy is inconsistent, the solution is almost always found in meal timing, carbohydrate intake, total calories, or sleep. Supplements should only be considered after these basics are already handled well.

When nutrition is built around real food, consistent structure, and adequate intake, supplements become optional tools rather than necessities. This aligns closely with the Norwegian philosophy: control the fundamentals, reduce unnecessary complexity, and allow performance to emerge from repeatable habits rather than shortcuts.

# THIRTY-SEVEN

# Bonus Chapter - The Secret Weapon

Among runners, treadmills often carry an unfair reputation. They are sometimes dismissed as easier, artificial, or somehow less legitimate than running outside. But when used intentionally, the treadmill is not a shortcut. It's a precision tool. And precision is exactly what structured endurance training demands.

The purpose of the Norwegian approach is not to chase dramatic workouts or prove toughness. It's to make quality sessions repeatable week after week. Outdoors, even the best-planned threshold run can quietly become sloppy. Small hills change your effort. Wind forces you to surge. Traffic lights break rhythm. Corners, crowds, and terrain constantly nudge your pace up or down. Each interruption seems minor, but together they turn what should be a controlled session into a series of mini accelerations and slowdowns. Instead of steady aerobic stress, you accumulate unnecessary fatigue.

The treadmill removes most of that noise. Once the speed is set, the pace simply stays there. You don't need to glance at your watch every few seconds or guess whether you are drifting too fast. You just settle into the effort and hold it. This makes threshold training cleaner and more controlled, which is the whole point. Threshold work is not meant to feel heroic or chaotic. It should feel steady, strong, and repeatable. Locking in a speed for ten, fifteen, or twenty minutes teaches exactly what that controlled discomfort feels like.

A common criticism is that treadmill running is easier than outside. In reality, it's simply different. Indoors there is no air resistance, fewer small terrain changes, and usually more consistent footing. To better match outdoor energy cost, many coaches recommend adding a small incline, with one percent being the most widely used rule of thumb. This modest adjustment brings effort closer to what you would experience on flat roads without turning the session into a climb. Cooling matters too. Warm indoor air can make workouts feel harder than they should. A simple fan aimed at your torso and face usually solves this and keeps effort comparable to outdoor running.

Setting up a treadmill session is straightforward. Use about one percent incline for most steady or threshold work. Warm up easily for ten to fifteen minutes, then gradually build speed over two to three minutes until you reach your target threshold pace. From there, focus on holding a steady, controlled effort rather than chasing numbers. The key rule is simple: if you cannot maintain the same breathing rhythm and sense of control from the middle of the interval to the end, the pace is too high.

If you're unsure what treadmill speed matches your personal threshold pace, you can quickly ask

ChatGPT to convert it for you. A simple prompt like "What treadmill speed equals my threshold pace?" will give you the exact setting to use, so you can focus on running by feel rather than guessing.

Beyond fitness gains, the treadmill offers something equally valuable: learning. Because the speed stays constant, you develop a clearer feel for different intensities. You begin to recognize the difference between easy running, steady aerobic work, and true threshold without relying on fluctuating terrain. When you repeat the same session weeks later, you can compare how controlled it feels rather than just how fast you went. This builds pacing discipline and confidence that transfer directly back to outdoor races.

Like any tool, treadmills work best when used strategically. They are ideal for one of your weekly quality sessions, especially threshold workouts where control matters most. They can also be helpful for steady aerobic segments when weather or traffic makes outdoor pacing difficult. They do not need to replace outdoor running. They simply add another reliable option that supports consistency.

In the end, the treadmill is not about convenience. It is about accuracy. And accuracy makes training repeatable. When sessions are repeatable, fitness compounds. That is why treadmills belong in a serious plan, not on the sidelines.

# Conclusion

By now, you've probably noticed something important about this approach.

There are no miracle workouts.

No secret intervals.

No "smash yourself into the ground" sessions that promise instant breakthroughs.

And that's the point.

The Norwegian method works not because it is extreme, but because it is repeatable.

Again and again throughout this book, the same ideas show up in different forms. Controlled threshold work. Easy running that stays easy. Long runs that build durability. Strength that supports movement. Sleep that allows recovery. Food that fuels the work. Small, steady progress layered over time.

None of these pieces are flashy on their own. But together, they create something powerful: consistency.

And consistency is what actually builds fitness.

A single hard week doesn't change your body much. A single perfect workout doesn't make you faster. What changes you is stacking hundreds of sensible sessions across months and years. It's showing up four or five or six days a week, doing the right work at the right effort, and finishing each session feeling like you could come back tomorrow and do it again.

That's how durable runners are built.

This is also why the system often feels almost "too simple." There's a natural temptation to search for something more complicated or more intense. To add extra workouts. To push every run. To look for shortcuts.

But most runners don't fail because they didn't train hard enough.

They fail because they couldn't stay healthy or consistent long enough.

Injuries. Burnout. Fatigue. Life stress. Starting and stopping.

The goal of this method is not to squeeze out one great race. It's to make sure you can train year-round without interruption. When you can do that, fitness compounds almost automatically.

Think of your training like building layers.

Each block adds a small layer of aerobic strength.

Each threshold session improves control and efficiency.

Each long run builds durability.

Each good night of sleep and solid meal helps you absorb the work.

Layer by layer, you become a stronger runner without dramatic jumps or risky gambles.

After a few months, you feel steadier.

After a year, you're noticeably fitter.

After several years, you're operating at a level that once felt out of reach.

Not because of one heroic effort, but because you simply never stopped.

As you move forward, remember that you don't need to follow these plans perfectly. Life will interrupt. Work will get busy. You'll miss days. You'll have weeks where everything feels off.

That's normal.

What matters is returning to the structure. Keep the principles simple. Keep the easy days easy. Keep threshold controlled. Protect recovery. Repeat what works.

When in doubt, choose the option you could sustain for the next six months, not the one that only works for a week.

Running is not a short project. It's a long relationship with your body.

Treat it with patience, respect the process, and trust that small, consistent steps add up.

If you do, the results will take care of themselves.

Now it's time to lace up and get back to work — one steady session at a time.

# References


Bompa, Tudor O., and Carlo Buzzichelli. Periodization: Theory and Methodology of Training. 6th ed. Champaign, IL: Human Kinetics, 2019.

Daniels, Jack. Daniels' Running Formula. 4th ed. Champaign, IL: Human Kinetics, 2021.

Fitzgerald, Matt. 80/20 Running: Run Stronger and Race Faster by Training Slower. New York: Penguin Random House, 2014.

Foster, Carl, Paul D. Lucia, and Jos J. de Koning. "Monitoring Training Load, Recovery, and Performance in Endurance Athletes." International Journal of Sports Physiology and Performance 12, no. 2 (2017): S2–S11.

Galloway, Jeff. Running Until You're 100. 2nd ed. Oxford: Meyer & Meyer Sport, 2017.

Hanson, Luke Humphrey. Hansons Marathon Method. Champaign, IL: Human Kinetics, 2014.

Joyner, Michael J., and Claude Bouchard. "Endurance Exercise Performance: The Physiology of Champions." Journal of Physiology 586, no. 1 (2008): 35–44.

Magness, Steve. The Science of Running. Houston: Origin Press, 2014.

McArdle, William D., Frank I. Katch, and Victor L. Katch. Exercise Physiology: Nutrition, Energy, and Human Performance. 9th ed. Philadelphia: Wolters Kluwer, 2022.

Midgley, Adrian W., and Lars R. McNaughton. "Time at or Near VO$_2$max During Continuous and Interval Training in Highly Trained Athletes." Journal of Sports Medicine 36, no. 2 (2006): 117–132.

Pfitzinger, Pete, and Scott Douglas. Advanced Marathoning. 3rd ed. Champaign, IL: Human Kinetics, 2019.

Rosekind, Mark R., Kevin B. Gregory, Melissa M. Mallis, Steven L. Brandt, Brian Seal, and Debra Lerner. "The NASA Nap Study: Alertness Management in Operational Settings." NASA Ames Research Center, 1995.

Seiler, Stephen, and Espen Tønnessen. "Intervals, Thresholds, and Long Slow Distance: The Role of Intensity and Duration in Endurance Training." Sportscience 13 (2009): 32–53.

Seiler, Stephen. "What Is Best Practice for Training Intensity and Duration Distribution in Endurance Athletes?" International Journal of Sports Physiology and Performance 5, no. 3 (2010): 276–291.

Skolnik, Matt. Build Your Running Body. New York: The Experiment, 2014.

Walker, Matthew. Why We Sleep: Unlocking the Power of Sleep and Dreams. New York: Scribner, 2017.

World Athletics. World Athletics Coaching Resources. Accessed February 10, 2026. https://www.worldathletics.org.

# Thanks for Reading!

I'm a coach, educator, and lifelong student of endurance performance. Over the years, I've helped runners at every level, from people training for their first 5K to experienced athletes chasing personal bests in the 10K and half marathon.

My coaching style is straightforward: train with intention, control intensity, and build fitness through consistency rather than constant suffering. Running isn't only about willpower or grinding through hard workouts. It's about repeatable training, smart progression, and learning how to work hard without tipping into fatigue that steals the next week.

This book was created to give you a clear, practical framework for training the Norwegian way—without needing elite genetics, unlimited time, or expensive testing. Each section is designed to help you understand what matters most, apply the principles in real life, and follow race-specific plans that build speed and endurance while protecting long-term health. The goal is not just a faster race, but a training system you can sustain for years.

If these pages help you train smarter and run better, I'd genuinely love to hear about it.

Scan the QR code to leave a quick Amazon review. Your feedback helps other runners discover the book, and it means a lot to me too.

Thanks for your support!

— Erik Lundqvist